MORE LIVES OF HARVARD SCHOLARS

A selection of biographies
written by their colleagues

Collected and arranged by
William Bentinck-Smith
and
Elizabeth Stouffer

HARVARD UNIVERSITY
OFFICE OF THE SECRETARY
CAMBRIDGE, MASSACHUSETTS
1986

For the portraits in the text we are indebted to Fabian
Bachrach—*Professor McIlwain*; John Brook—*Professors
Elisséeff, Gropius, MacLeish, Piston, Richards, Rosenberg*;
Harvard Law Art Collection—*Professors Fuller, Hart*;
Patricia Hollander—*Professor Howe*; Milton Machálek—
Professor Perkins; The Marshall Studio—*Professor Williams*.
Other portraits are from the Harvard University Archives,
the Business School Archives, and the Medical Area News
Office.

CONTENTS

FOREWORD

This anthology of Harvard biography gets its inspiration from a paperback volume published in 1968 under the auspices of the Harvard Information Center for circulation at a very modest price to visitors and members of the Harvard community. The small printing was soon exhausted, and the book is now an item of some rarity, but a lasting tribute to the caring hand of its principal anonymous editor, William M. Pinkerton.

The present volume begins where the other left off and, following a similar somewhat random and arbitrary arrangement, gathers between its buckram covers 38 biographical sketches chosen from among more than 200 memoirs of Harvard scholars who died in the past two decades. The task of selection has not been easy, and the editors are grateful to the deans of the several faculties and their associates who considered the project and made suggestions—but bear no responsibility for the final result. In the end the choices had to become a subjective editorial judgment based in part on each individual's distinction, memorable character or contributions to Harvard life, and in part on the literary quality of the selection. Most of the memoirs were culled from the files of the Faculty of Arts and Sciences and bear testimony to the traditional high standard of these tributes. In the case of faculties which do not normally adopt memorial minutes, such as those of Law and Business, the editors have gone to other sources, when available, even though the essay may not contain all the factual material normally included in the statement of a faculty committee. There were several individuals who could not be represented simply because no sufficient sketch yet existed.

We can only hope that the families and admirers of the scores who might have been included in this selection will make allowance for the difficulty of choosing. If they can forgive omissions obvious and inevitable, we hope the lives and achievements recalled in this little volume will be a reminder of the splendor, quality and variety of the continuing collective effort of this great university as it celebrates its 350th birthday.

In addition to the deans, many contributed to the final compilation. First among them were Robert Shenton, Secretary to the Governing Boards and to the University; Barbara B. Ford, Associate Secretary; Kathryn Urcda, Staff Assistant; Phyllis Keller, Associate Dean of the Faculty of Arts and Sciences; and Barbara M. Baker, Manager of the University Information Center, who suggested the project. The final burden of searching out memoirs and photographs fell on the shoulders of Robin McElheny of the University Archives (who supervised the reproduction of the portraits); Margery Heffron and Grace W. Choi of the University News Office; Barbara Steiner of the Medical Area News Office; Florence Bartoshesky of the Business School Archives; Bernice S. Loss, Curator of the Art Collections, Law School Library; and Anne F. Lessels of the Office of the Secretary of the Faculty of Arts and Sciences. To all of them warmest thanks, as well as to the able and efficient Daniel J. McCarron, Associate University Publisher, and Daniel J. Griffin, Publications Editor, who designed and planned the volume.

Although we hope this book will be read and appreciated by many outside as well as inside Harvard, it is particularly intended as a memento for the several thousand sons and daughters of the University who were chosen as special representatives of their colleges and schools to attend Harvard's 350th anniversary celebration in September 1986. To them it brings the University's special thanks and good wishes.

William Bentinck-Smith
Elizabeth Stouffer

I. The Written Word

HUMANIST

"The best that has been thought and said"

JOHN NASH DOUGLAS BUSH

March 21, 1896 - March 1, 1983

Douglas Bush, one of the fore-most humanists of our century, was born in Morrisburg, Ontario. His father, Dexter Bush, devoted 60 hours a week to managing a small dry-goods store; but he hated the business and, in spare moments, turned for relief to writing light comic verse with elegance and wit. His gift for well-turned phrasing was caught by the boy, whose writing and lectures, however serious the subject, were throughout his life graced by wit and humor.

Like so many writers and scholars born in the Victorian period, Bush's interest in literature was inspired by the family custom of reading aloud. His mother, Mary Nash Bush, read nightly to her children from the great Victorian novelists. They especially enjoyed the marvelous comic scenes in Charles Dickens.

By his early teens, Douglas had devoured most of the famous children's books, among them the historical tales of G.A. Henty, which gave him a love of history. When he was 15, he used $10 he had saved from hard work to buy second-hand the completed works of Macaulay and read them through, including not only the *History of*

3

England and the historical and literary essays, but also the formidable discussion of the Indian Penal Code. From Macaulay he moved on to other historians, and to the lives and works of great statesmen, particularly Edmund Burke. All his life Bush retained a special interest in masters of thinking prose, in whom eloquence and strength of language were combined with knowledge, practical insight, and imaginative vision.

In all of the 21 examinations then demanded for entrance to the University of Toronto, he passed with distinction. Having already at school studied Greek and Latin for six years, he concentrated in classical literature, history, and philosophy, graduating in 1920 and taking an M.A. in these subjects the next year.

So broadly humanistic was his approach, seeking what his admired Mathew Arnold described as "the best that has been thought and said" throughout humanity's experience, that Bush—already an accomplished scholar in the classics—found himself repelled by what he called the "aridity" of professional classical scholarship. It seemed to suffer, he said, from a "detached retina," focusing on minute problems of philology, grammar, and textual editing. English literature, he naively thought, so he said, might be more broadly open to humanistic study and teaching. Having only enough money for two years of graduate study, he applied in 1921 to the Harvard English department. He received a shock when he learned that, of the 16 courses he had to take, all but two consisted of medieval languages and philology (including not only Anglo-Saxon, and the various dialects of Middle English and Middle Scots, but also Old French, Gothic, and other recondite tongues).

From the beginning, this great liberal was also a conservative: he believed in working from within in order to improve things and not simply kicking the outworks of the Bastille. Gritting his teeth, he passed all of these courses at the top of his class, afterwards burning his books, especially his Gothic grammar, with great gusto. At the same time, he passed his doctoral oral with the

highest distinction, and finished a magisterial thesis on
Mythology and the Renaissance Tradition, more accurately
described as Renaissance reconsideration of its classical
inheritance and later published in a book (1932) that is
still regarded as the standard work.

All of this he accomplished in two years. Naturally
impressed, his teachers, whatever the implied criticism
against themselves, recommended him for the position
of instructor and tutor in 1923, a title that was higher
at the time than at present. Four years later (1927), when
Bush was 31, he was made assistant professor at the
University of Minnesota, where, after one year, he was
promoted to tenure and in another two years made
chairman of the department.

When Bush returned to Harvard at the age of 40, it
was to an English department which, however still distinguished, was more seriously divided than it has been
at any time during its long history. In the then conservative faction were the champions of philology and old-
fashioned literary history. In its left wing were the champions of everything that seemed to differ from these,
ranging from history of ideas, in which literature was
treated as a branch of intellectual history, through soci-
ological and political interpretations, to what was later
called the New Criticism, which sought to diminish
historial, social, and intellectual contexts in favor of a
more exclusive concentration on the native texts. Bush
offered a different alternative: the classical and Renaissance ideal of *litterae humaniores*, which drew on all the
major approaches and subsumed them into a broader
humanism, moral as well as intellectual. Important publications at this time included his comprehensive *Mythology
and the Romantic Tradition* (1937), which could more justly
be entitled, "The Poetic Mind of England and Its Use of
the Classical Inheritance" from the close of the Renaissance to the twentieth century.

In the years after World War II, Harvard quickly
became aware that it had in Bush a humanist and scholar
of world reputation. In the courses he gave, alternating

them from year to year (Renaissance literature, Milton, the great Romantic poets, the nineteenth-century novel, and seminars in several more specialized subjects) the enrollment quintupled, though his lecture delivery was low-keyed and deliberately undramatic. At times it seemed that a third of the large number of postwar graduate students were writing theses under him; and scores of them, by the 1950s and 1960s, were to occupy key positions in literary departments throughout the land.

Every week we would see him departing from Warren House with an armful of theses or a bundle of manuscripts from former students, now professors elsewhere, asking for criticism. He never complained. He never asked for secretarial help to handle the huge number of recommendations he was requested to write. Throughout the night he would type these out himself. In addition, visting scholars from every country in Europe or the Orient would flock to his door with manuscripts to read or to review. He could never say no to any of them.

Meanwhile, his own books kept appearing. His great history of *English Literature in the Seventeenth Century* (1945), written for the then new series of the Oxford History, set so high an example that other scholars, writing other volumes, felt that they could not match it and gave up, with the result that the series was left unfinished. Other works included two books on Milton (1945 and 1964), a history of English poetry from Chaucer to the present (1952), *Science and English Poetry* (1950), *Prefaces to Renaissance Literature* (1965), his charming collection of essays, *Engaged and Disengaged* (1966), and a variety of other books, including standard editions of Keats, Tennyson, and especially Milton.

At the same time he was turning out magnificent manifestoes in defense of the humanities, in their broad and classical sense. Harvard scientists loved him for this; and for 30 years he was one of the key humanists, by their own choice, in that select body known as the Cambridge Scientific Club. They, like everyone else who knew him, were delighted by his quiet and ready wit, which appeared even in casual conversations.

Of the many anecdotes, we have room for only one. The British novelist C. P. Snow visited Harvard not long after he published his novel *The Masters*, which had fascinated American academics with its account of the elaborate and tortuous deals, counterdeals, intrigues and realignments in the election of the master of a Cambridge college. Bush, on being introduced, beamed at Snow and said cheerfully, "Your book *The Masters* is the only thing I ever read that *completely* reconciled me to Harvard's system of autocratic appointments."

Another characteristic of Bush was his phenomenal memory. It is true, for example, that he knew *Paradise Lost* by heart, a poem of about 11,000 lines. After a train trip to Chicago in the 1940s, when he had to speak at a convention, one of us asked him how he whiled away the time on the train, for we knew he disliked traveling. He replied that he recited *Paradise Lost* silently to himself. "Did it see you through the trip?' he was asked. "No. I tried to go slowly, but I found it took only nine hours. It carried me about as far as Utica."

Bush, all his life, dreaded publicity and acclaim. It was characteristic of him that, in his final year of teaching in 1966, he concluded his courses a week before the official end of the term in order to avoid the applause and, to him, embarrassing attention shown to professors in their last lecture. Typically, this pre-eminent humanist also before he retired resigned his small Widener study, in order to make room for younger people on the waiting list for these rooms.

In his 70s, after retirement, Bush continued to be active, publishing five more books on a variety of authors and subjects, all of them penetrating, if brief, and sprinkled with his usual wit. Manuscripts continued to arrive at his door for evaluation, all of them returned in a few days, with detailed comments and generous understanding. Needless to say, in his many years of teaching, his tender-heartedness as well as his openness of mind had made him the victim not only of brilliant former students who continued into late middle-age to ask for help, but also of innumerable cranks, waifs, and strays, who demanded advice and support. Quietly through the night hours, Bush in his 70s and early 80s continued to go over their work with the same care, it seems, as that which he would give to the work of noted scholars also requesting his help.

And forever, despite his immense learning and his sharp, unrivaled accuracy of judgment, he was among the humblest of great men, completely lacking in anything that savored of vanity or self-importance; and the exacting daily summonses that life gives to the conscientious seem to have been felt by him not merely as a duty but a privilege as well. When he died just short of his 87th birthday, all of us thought that of no one we knew could the biblical quotation applied to another professor, who died over a century ago, be so appropriate now: that, in all his years here, he walked among us and "wist not that his face shone."

Herschel Baker	Paul Freund
Jerome Buckley	Walter Kaiser
John Finley	David Perkins

W. Jackson Bate, *Chairman*

Memorial Minute
Faculty of Arts and Sciences
May 17, 1983

POET

"He fell in love with Harvard"
ARCHIBALD MacLEISH
May 7, 1892 - March 20, 1982

Archibald MacLeish, who died shortly before his 90th birthday, rejoined the Harvard faculty in 1949—and in a sense remained in spirit with us, in the almost 20 years since his retirement at 70, in May 1962. For he retained an eager and informed interest in Harvard during those years of retirement, knew everything that was happening in his beloved English department, kept abreast of the more gifted young, and continued to view Harvard as his spiritual home.

There are at least two things about this remarkable man that were almost unique. For one thing, he did not seem to age. When he was 63 and served as acting master of Eliot House, during one of John Finley's rare absences, he asked the chairman of this committee (26 years younger) to take an afternoon stroll along the river to Mt. Auburn and back. We did this rapidly, and when we returned Archie was breathing health and joy, while his much younger colleague found himself panting with fatigue. When he retired at 70, which he resented deeply though quietly, he could seem a healthy 50. So up to his

9

85th year, when, for the first time, he suddenly began to strike people as a possible 70 or 75.

This may not be completely unique. But another fact about him is, at least among men of letters and anyone else we have known personally. This was his astonishing range of talent and expertise: law, government, business, publishing, agriculture, humanist in general; and, what meant most to him, he was one of the half-dozen leading poets of his generation—a very brilliant generation in poetry, which has set a hard example to poets who have followed.

We can give only the briefest summary of a career so richly varied in talent and achievement. He was born in Glencoe, Illinois, the son of Andrew and Martha Hilliard MacLeish. The father had emigrated from Scotland as a boy, and, in one of the classic stories of immigrants, had risen to the managership of one of Chicago's great department stores—Carson, Pirie, Scott, and Company.

His mother, Martha Hilliard, came from an old New England family. Her father and several ancestors had been Congregational ministers. After attending local schools at Glencoe, and then Hotchkiss School, Archie entered Yale, as his mother's male ancestors had, and graduated in 1915, becoming a member of Phi Beta Kappa at the same time. He was also a leading member of the football and swimming teams. He then entered Harvard Law School where he graduated in 1919 at the very top of his class, receiving the Fay Prize given to the outstanding scholar. His student days were interrupted by service in the Field Artillery during World War I, in which he rose quickly from private to captain. Shortly after the close of World War I, he taught constitutional law here for two years. One of our most distinguished economists, Edward Mason, took this course and remembers Archie's dialectical brilliance; and others have said the same of this course. MacLeish also served in the Boston law office of Charles Choate for three years. But his great desire, still, was to devote himself to poetry. And having recently married Ada Hitchcock—already an accomplished singer, and later remembered by so many of us as one of the notable Cambridge hostesses, when she and Archie returned in 1949—he went off with his family to Europe, living in Paris, Italy, and, for a while, Persia.

In the 1920s he became known as one of the famous expatriates (like T. S. Eliot, Ezra Pound, Gertrude Stein, Hemingway, and others). He wrote prolifically, but the call of America grew on him with every year, and a kind of gradual disgust—especially later on—for what he felt was the "escapism" of the so-called "lost generation." Then began a new period in his writing. Returning in 1928, he traveled for months through Mexico, by mule track, retracing the route of the explorer Hernando Cortes, and later published a long poem, *The Conquistador* (1932), which won him the first of the three Pulitzer Prizes he received. Meanwhile, he had become editor of Henry Luce's new magazine, *Fortune*, for which he wrote brilliantly on every conceivable subject and became widely regarded as one of the most active liberal writers of the 1930s. To list the variety of subjects, and the groups of liberal intellectuals that he headed or helped, would use up more space than we can here give. The Depression deepened both his political liberalism and his general patriotism. About this time—and certainly in the 1940s till the end of his life, he loved (like a Roman of the age of Cato) to refer to the country as "the Republic." The word brought up all the semantic associations with the American past—the Founding Fathers, the drama of the early American Republic, the associations with Rome before the Empire, and with figures like Washington, Jefferson, and Lincoln.

In 1938, MacLeish was appointed by President Conant to serve as curator for the Nieman Fellows. But within another year, Franklin Roosevelt asked him to serve as Librarian of Congress, a job he held for five years. Concurrently, during World War II, he served as director of the Office of Facts and Figures and assistant director of the Office of War Information, and later (1944-45) as assistant secretary of state, when he helped to plan the

11

United Nations Educational, Scientific and Cultural Organization (Unesco).

When a committee, chaired by Harry Levin, recommended him as the new Boylston Professor of Rhetoric and Oratory, in 1949, he was naturally appointed, though President Conant is reputed to have said, "I'll be surprised if he stays two years." But Archie fell in love with Harvard, as no one we have known who has come to us at that age. He told us that he took the job, partly because of the title, Boylston Professor of Rhetoric and Oratory, which reminded him of the early days of the Republic. He became an intimate of President Pusey, as he already was with Dean Bundy, and the department rejoiced that we had a friend in court for the first time in two decades. He taught a brilliant large lecture course, modestly called "An Approach to Poetry," and also gave the most advanced course in composition (or writing). After a few years, he made a special arrangement with the administration to teach half-time—one term per year—in order to have more leisure to write. He spent much of the winter in Antigua, in the West Indies, and the rest of his free time at his home—a beautiful old farmhouse, much enlarged, in Conway, Massachusetts, which the MacLeishes had bought and remodeled in the 1920s. But he was in constant consultation with the English department, to which he returned when important business was afoot. He also chaired the committee on dramatics at the crucial time when funds were being collected for the Loeb Drama Center.

Meanwhile, other honors came to him—a second Pulitzer for his *Collected Poems* in 1953. Then, when he retired, he received a third Pulitzer for a play, *J.B.*— based on the biblical story of Job, but put in a modern setting. In addition to other plays, he wrote books about the use and importance of the humanities, all of them eloquent and persuasive.

Active until his 89th year, he began to fail at last in the winter of 1981-82. He entered Massachusetts General

Hospital on March 20, 1982, for what was found to be cancer. He died on April 20.

William Alfred   Walter Kaiser
John Conway   Harry Levin
John Finley   David Perkins
                W. Jackson Bate, *Chairman*

Memorial Minute
Faculty of Arts and Sciences
February 15, 1983

LITERARY CRITIC

"Impeccable scholar, invigorating teacher"

ISABEL GAMBLE MacCAFFREY

August 2, 1924 - May 19, 1978

The facts of Isabel Gamble MacCaffrey's bright but brief career may be quickly told. The daughter of Dr. Thomas O. and Isabel (Davidson) Gamble of Albany, New York, she began her education at the Girls Academy in that city, took her first degree at Swarthmore in 1946, and the next fall entered  Radcliffe to study for the PH.D. In 1949 an instructorship in English inaugurated her long and affectionate association with Bryn Mawr College, where—after time off for a Fulbright fellowship at Cambridge in 1950-51 and a Radcliffe PH.D. in 1954—she rose serenely up the academic ladder to a full professorship in 1966. In 1959, three years after her marriage to Wallace MacCaffrey, the publication of her remarkable *Paradise Lost as Myth* earned for her a reputation that was duly signalized by a stream of honorific appointments: election to the supervisory committee of the English Institute in 1967, a fellowship at Girton College in 1968, a Guggenheim fellowship in 1971, a seat on the editorial board of PMLA (Proceedings of the Modern Language Association) and a fellowship at New Hall, Cambridge, in 1975 and honorary degrees at

Holy Cross and Smith in 1973 and 1978. On her hus-
band's move from Haverford to Harvard she was named
to a professorship at Tufts in 1969, and two years later
to the Kenan chair at Harvard. Here in what was to be
the final phase of her career, she quickly made her vital
presence felt, not only in the Department of English and
in the committee on history and literature but also as a
syndic of the Harvard Press, an associate of Lowell House,
an acting senior fellow in the Society of Fellows, and a
brisk and forceful member of many departmental and
university committees. With a gallant disregard for
failing health—and despite her heavy duties in teaching
and administration—in 1976 she crowned her long
devotion to Renaissance literature with her masterful
study of *Spencer's Allegory*. A projected work on English
philosophical poetry was cut short by her untimely death.

To record the routine facts of an illustrious career—
degrees conferred, books published, appointments secured,
honors bestowed—is an easy ceremonial gesture on occasions such as this, but to convey something of Isabel
MacCaffrey's peculiar strength and charm requires that
we recapture, if we can, her most uncommon blend of
delicacy with power, of mind with feeling, of an impe-
rious and sometimes ruthless intellect with a compassionate response to frailty and failure, of the most
fastidious scholarship with stunning flights of intuition,
of unblinking professional probity with a gourmet's skill
in cooking. Binding these and many such antitheses
together was a monolithic strength of character that
found expression in a roguish grin and that was rooted
in a salty sense of humor. High spirited, quick, and
witty, she loved to banter—at times hilariously—about
the quirks of academic potentates and the foibles of the
would-be great, for which she had a piercing and unerring
eye. An impeccable scholar and an invigorating teacher
free of pretense, she worked effectively within the boundaries of her own capacious skills. Her invincible integrity
was stamped like a signature on everything she did or
wrote. Invulnerable to the customary disabilities of ego-

tism, pride, and prickly sensitivity, she was also undaunted by pain and sickness and misfortune. Fortified by her formidable intelligence (to say nothing of her robust common sense and valor), she looked at the world cheerfully, hopefully, and a little wryly, and she was prepared for almost anything.

It was well that this was so, for her appointment as chairman of the committee on history and literature required that she *had* to be prepared. Her adroit management of the students, tutors, and professors, in a field where delicate sensibilities tend to be as common as high intelligence, will remain a model of luck and pluck and academic cunning. Drawing on her deep reserves of patience, wit, and candor, she not only kept the peace; she also played a decisive role in negotiations that enlarged the scope and functions of this small but vital field of concentration.

The skillful academic politician was also one of the most perceptive scholar-critics of her generation. Although her lesser things—which range from the Elizabethans through Marvell and Wordsworth to Wallace Stevens—reveal the working of a mind both supple and profound, it is for her full-length books on the two greatest narrative and philosophical poems in our language—*Paradise Lost* and *The Faerie Queene*—that she will most likely be remembered. With their easy authority over voluminous and challenging materials, their strength of structure, and their wonderful lucidity of style these works stand proudly eminent in the swarm of modern studies of the English Renaissance; but they rise even higher for their boldness of conception and their range of speculation on the ways a poet's thinking is expressed in language and on the kind of knowledge it conveys.

These books, like Isabel MacCaffrey's whole career, exemplify a quality of mind and character that, as noted in the citation of her posthumous honorary degree from Smith, Milton recognized as "of a quick, ingenious and piercing spirit, acute to invent, subtle and sinewy to discourse, not beneath the reach of any point the highest that human capacity can soar to." To all who knew Isabel MacCaffrey, the relevance is clear.

Bernard Bailyn   John Clive
Warner Berthoff   Herschel Baker, *Chairman*

Memorial Minute
Faculty of Arts and Sciences
October 16, 1979

SCHOLAR OF JAPAN

"A new era in Asian studies"

SERGE ELISSÉEFF

January 13, 1889 - April 13, 1975

Serge Elisséeff was born in St.
Petersburg, the third son of a
wealthy family of peasant origin
which had become famous
purveyors of wines and delica-
cies. He was tutored in French,
German, and English, and
instructed in Latin and Greek
at the Karlinsky lycée from
which he graduated in 1907 at
the head of his class. By then he was also an avid student
of painting and an admirer of Chinese and Japanese art,
which he had discovered in visiting the Paris World
Exposition of 1900 during a summer at the family resi-
dence in Neuilly. Having been advised to give up an
artistic career, since his background precluded the sup-
posedly necessary suffering, he accepted the further
advice to study Chinese and Japanese for two years at the
University of Berlin and then proceed to Tokyo to prepare
himself to be the first fully qualified European Japanologist.

At the age of 19, though armed with impressive letters
of introduction, Elisséeff was somewhat reluctantly
admitted to Tokyo Imperial University as its first regular
student from the mysterious West. He began a full program of academic work, sustained by Japanese tutors

18

whom he employed from 8 a.m. to 8 p.m. seven days a week, to make up for the deficiencies of his earlier education. He nevertheless found time to become a connoisseur of Kabuki and an accomplished performer of theatrical recitation and dance. Among his friends were leading writers, actors, and geisha; his expertise in the arts ranged from calligraphy to comic storytelling. Far from neglecting his studies, he wrote an ambitious thesis in Japanese on the poetry of Bashō, and did so well in the final oral examination on Japanese language and literature that he was in the front row of honor graduates in 1912. The commencement exercises were attended by the Meiji emperor, his last public appearance before his death, and Elisséeff always humorously averred that the shock of seeing a Western face in the group hastened the emperor's demise.

After six years in Tokyo, Serge Elisséeff went home in the summer of 1914 to begin fulfilling the requirements for an obligatory PH.D. at the University of Petrograd. Later that year he married Vera Eiche, who was his lifelong companion until her death in 1971. Both his private fortune and the nearly completed manuscript of his Russian doctoral dissertation were casualties of the Bolshevik revolution, but Elisséeff remained active in the perilous academic life of Petrograd until 1920, when, after near starvation and frequent harassment, he escaped in a fishing boat with his wife and two small sons to Finland.

In January 1921, the Elisséeffs came to Paris, surviving at first by selling family jewels they had secreted in a medicine bottle. Various work for the Japanese embassy led, most congenially, to translating modern Japanese literature and writing lengthy scholarly reviews for the monthly *Japon et Extrême-Orient*, which soon expired from withdrawal of the support of its business sponsors. Most of Elisséeff's later writing was in the field of art history. Meanwhile he had begun teaching Japanese literature at the Sorbonne, and by 1932 he held a chair in the religions section of the École Pratique des Hautes Études.

A new era in the development of Asian studies in the United States began when Elisséeff, who had spent 1932-33 at Harvard as a visiting professor, was invited to return in 1934 as professor of Far Eastern languages and the first director of the Harvard-Yenching Institute. For over two decades he devoted much of his time and energy to supervising the institute's activities in East Asia and at Harvard, where the steady growth of instruction, research, and publication was complemented by that of the Chinese-Japanese Library. But he always took special pleasure in teaching. He gave generously of his time for individual reading courses, and lectured regularly on the history or literature of Japan from 11 a.m. until 12:30 p.m. on Tuesdays and Thursdays, often carrying on with characteristic wit and warmth, and with unflagging zest, until reminded of lunch by the tolling of the one o'clock bell.

Elisséeff shared the aspirations and precise philological methods of French Sinology—he once declared the wish "to create in this country a Sinology as outstanding as, for example, astronomy, where Americans have eminent men"—and he was also determined to prepare American scholars to cope with the esoteric problems of Japanese studies. It is perhaps regrettable that some of his particular abilities, such as his gift for literary translation and for impeccable *haute vulgarisation*, were sacrificed to his concept of a scientific "Japanology," his ever-increasing administrative burdens, and his self-imposed obligation to write and teach in a language twice-removed from the natural ease of the monolingual. "I am usually thinking in French," he sometimes remarked ruefully, "but when I am tired I am thinking in Russian."

In 1957 he returned with Mme. Elisséeff to the Paris apartment which they had steadfastly maintained along with their French citizenship. For seven more years he lectured at the Sorbonne. Even in his last years, confined to a wheelchair, Elisséeff continued to astonish visitors from Japan with his elegant calligraphy and fluent,

Meiji-era Japanese, as well as with his irrepressible sense of humor.

Among his many honors were two given him by the Japanese: the Order of the Sacred Treasure in 1968 and, in 1973, the first Japan Foundation Award in the category of "foreign individuals who have helped to explain Japan and Japanese culture to their own nations." Ironically, Serge Elisséeff's work was to benefit Europe and America more than his native Russia. But there can be no doubt of the depth of his influence, and of the affection and admiration in which his memory is held by his many students here and abroad.

Francis W. Cleaves Donald H. Shively
Edwin O. Reischauer Lien-sheng Yang
Howard S. Hibbett, *Chairman*

Memorial Minute
Faculty of Arts and Sciences
April 12, 1977

21

II. Past and Present

HISTORIAN OF WAR
AND PEACE

*"His studies have been a standard
for forty years"*

WILLIAM LEONARD LANGER

March 16, 1896 - December 26, 1977

Disturbed by students' inability in the late 1960s to find their identity, William L. Langer was moved to write his autobiography. Believing with the immigrant families of his generation that America was still a land of freedom and opportunity, he harked back to the events of his childhood and
youth. It was his last book—*In and Out of the Ivory Tower*—and a copy reached him just before he died, in his 82nd year. Even those who thought they knew him well found much to surprise them and much to explain his extraordinary career.

Born in South Boston, he was the second of three sons of Charles Rudolph and Johanna (Rockenbach) Langer, both recently arrived in this country from Germany. The father was prospering, but he died suddenly when the boy was three years old, leaving Mrs. Langer pregnant with their third son and without money. She supported and cared for the three boys, taking boarders and working as a dressmaker to make ends meet. Langer affectionately recalls a Spartan but happy childhood: good food, demanding household chores, and—from the age of nine onward—a series of part-time jobs. And always there was school. The third-grade teacher with the rattan cane that hurt his hand nonetheless interested Langer in history, geography, and spelling. Afterwards came the Boston Latin School, an arduous three-mile walk, and then Harvard, worlds away from South Boston, though only an hour by the newly completed subway. Determined to be practical, Langer concentrated in modern languages instead of in the history and classics that had become his real interest. As for student life, he noted, "I simply did not have it."

In his freshman year, Langer got high marks in seven courses. When the dean maintained that this was impossible, Langer won the argument by pointing out that he had done it. He also hypnotized the dean into admitting Rudolph Langer, the eldest brother, who had left high school to help support the family. Rudolph got four A's his freshman year and became a distinguished mathematician. The third son, Walter Langer, later became a psychoanalyst. Without Langer's autobiography, one could not have imagined the inspiring story of his youth, his own role in his brothers' careers, and behind all three youngsters the indomitable figure of Mrs. Langer.

Receiving his A.B. in 1915, Langer taught German for two years at Worcester Academy. With the First World War under way, intensely curious about its origins, and already Wilsonian in his thinking, he simultaneously studied international relations at Clark University. In December 1917, he enlisted, serving in France in a chemical warfare unit whose history he wrote immediately after the Armistice: his first book. Then he returned to Harvard as a graduate student in history—"a subject," he said, "every aspect of which aroused my interest and engaged my thought." Archibald Cary Coolidge, the first scholar in America to see the importance of studying Russian, Near Eastern, and Asian history, became his mentor and close personal friend. Langer did research for his PH.D. thesis in the imperial archives of Vienna during the frigid winter of 1921-22 and studied Russian on the side. He received the PH.D. degree in 1923 and, after four years teaching modern European history at Clark, he returned to Harvard as assistant professor. When Professor Coolidge died early in 1928, Langer succeeded to his course on the Near Eastern question, dealing with the Ottoman empire and its many subject peoples, Christian and Muslim, viewing Europe from Constantinople, and assessing the centuries-long diplomatic and military impact of the Turks on international affairs. Every year, Langer also lectured on modern European history from 1815 to 1914. In 1931, he became associate professor and in 1936 the first incumbent of the Coolidge chair, founded by his beloved teacher's own bequest. Nothing could have given Langer greater pleasure or have been more appropriate.

As a lecturer, Langer was easy, fluent, pungent, his material lucidly organized, each sentence ending on a curious rising tone at the moment where other men's voices drop, a style that tempted successive generations of undergraduates to efforts at imitation. In his autobiography, Langer later described the sudden attacks of "stage-fright," beginning in 1938, that beset him while lecturing, and turned each class into a nightmare for him. Such was his iron control, however, and so unaffected was his actual performance that this revelation astounded even colleagues who had taught courses jointly with him and attended all his lectures.

Langer's seminar met in the evening in his own study at home, the students working within a field of modern diplomatic history so circumscribed that all could gain a general acquaintance with the source materials and the monographic literature. Each student would deliver his report orally and submit to criticism first by all the other students and finally by Langer himself. Woe betide the young scholar whose report seemed to neglect some useful avenue of approach: once, when all the student critics

27

had offered admiring comments on a report, and Langer's turn came, he said to the author, "Well, Mr. X, it is a pretty good paper, but did you use the Italian sources?" When X replied, "But Mr. Langer, I don't read Italian," Langer's ringing rejoinder was "How do you know Mr. X? Have you ever tried?" By lunchtime next day, this reply was reverberating among the graduate students in history and has continued to echo down the ages. Langer subjected the final written papers to the most searching scrutiny: a rigorous professional training for future professionals. On seminar evenings themselves, however, Mrs. Langer appeared in the doorway at 10, with beer and coffee. Discussion would become general, and relaxation would set in.

Langer's writings had the same magisterial quality as his teaching. His monograph on *The Franco-Russian Alliance, 1890-1894* (1929) explored the first stages in the unraveling of Bismarck's system of alliances, the rapprochement between Tsarist Russia at one of its most reactionary moments and the French Third Republic at one of its most liberal ones. *European Alliances and Alignments, 1870-1890* (1931) described the building of the intricate Bismarckian system of security down to the Kaiser's dismissal of its architect in 1890. *The Diplomacy of Imperialism* in two volumes (1935) carried the subject down to 1902, into an era when friction was replacing equilibrium. Langer performed a prodigious amount of research, using all the appropriate languages, and then achieved a splendidly organized, clearly written, and almost preternatually objective, even detached, treatment of the complex material. Unlike any other historical studies of their scope, these books have remained standard for more than 40 years.

With the Japanese, Italian, and German aggression of the mid and late thirties, Langer turned his attention to current developments, writing shorter articles for a wider audience. Many appeared in *Foreign Affairs*, the magazine of the Council on Foreign Relations, in whose pages during the 11 years between 1925 and 1936 Langer had

28

written brief incisive comment on approximately 600 new books a year. With the help of other scholars during the 1930s, Langer wholly revised Ploetz's *Epitome of History*, which reappeared in 1940 as *An Encyclopaedia of World History* and is still going strong in its fifth edition. He also undertook the planning and editorship of a 20-volume series on the Rise of Modern Europe, reserving for himself a volume on the two decades between 1832 and 1852.

As World War II moved into its most threatening phases, President Roosevelt in the summer of 1941 appointed Colonel William J. Donovan as chief of the first United States coordinated foreign intelligence service in our history. Langer became deputy chief and then chief of the research and analysis branch of this agency, by 1942 known as the Office of Strategic Services. The R and A branch became as large as a university faculty, with its own offices overseas and its members attached to offices of other OSS branches.

The analysts worried about the effectiveness of their work and often grumbled because it seldom drew immediate audible applause. Once, Langer called them together and encouraged them, using a metaphor from his own experience in World War I, "If one shot in 10 hits anything worth hitting," he declared, "the artillery's doing fine." The mere sight of him and the sound of that gravelly voice did some good, but the discovery some weeks later that the R and A study of North African seaports had played an essential part in the American landings in Africa did much more. Now wholly declassified, the work of Langer's branch can be judged by students of the United States in World War II.

In autumn, 1943, Cordell Hull, Secretary of State, invited Langer to write a study of American wartime relations with the French, offering free access to all the documents. Continuing to run the R and A branch all day, he now spent two to three hours every evening at the State Department. His book, *Our Vichy Gamble*, appeared in 1947. Its soundness as a work of history compelled even those who vehemently disliked its message to treat it more respectfully than he had expected. In 1946, Langer undertook, with the collaboration of S. Everett Gleason, to write for the Council on Foreign Relations a history of American policy during World War II. Undeterred by the *Chicago Tribune*, which called him a "hired liar," in 1952 and 1953 he and Gleason produced two massive and lucid volumes, *The Challenge to Isolation, 1937-1940* and *The Undeclared War, 1940-1941*, which remain the basic account of American foreign policy in the years before Pearl Harbor. But Langer had to stop there. As he put it, "The writing of contemporary history is like the work of Sisyphus."

In 1950, Langer obtained an additional year of leave to organize the office of national estimates in the newly established Central Intelligence Agency. But except for membership after 1961 on the President's Foreign Intelligence Advisory Board, the year 1952 marked the end of Langer's government service. He was awarded the Medal for Merit by President Truman in 1945. It would be hard to think of any productive scholar-historian who ever made so extensive a contribution to government in war and peace.

Back at Harvard in the early fifties, Langer became intimately connected with the regional studies programs and their affiliated research centers, established for Russia and East Asia after the war. In 1954, he was instrumental in founding the new Center for Middle Eastern studies, and in 1955 became director of the Russian Research Center and chairman of the entire regional studies effort. These enterprises still flourish and owe him a debt of gratitude.

Langer's deep curiosity about men and affairs turned in the fifties and sixties to new fields of inquiry. As president of the American Historical Association, he delivered at Christmas 1957 an address on the importance of depth psychology as a tool for historians seeking to explain human motivation. He discussed in some detail the childhood and youth of Martin Luther and argued that, if one had correspondence or diaries written by an author with no inkling that it might be read with psychical analysis in mind, one should make judicious analytical use of it. After the address, which came as a bombshell, Langer learned that Erik Erikson was working on a full-length analytical study of Luther, which Erikson then invited him to read in proof. Langer also asked whether psychoanalytical techniques could be helpful to historians in their study of larger currents of history, such as, for example, the aftermath of great plagues like the Black Death of 1348-1349. This brilliant portion of the address, discussing the impact of the plague on religion, art and literature, went almost unnoticed. Langer next explored demography and related Europe's first population explosion to the spreading cultivation of the potato. In 1969, his former student, Professor Carl Schorske of Princeton, and Mrs. Schorske edited a volume of Langer's previously uncollected papers called *Exploration in Crisis*, with a fine introductory appreciation. In the same year Langer published his own often-postponed volume in his own series on the Rise of Modern Europe, *Political and Social Upheaval, 1832-1852*.

Honors naturally poured in upon Langer. He cherished his membership in the American Philosophical Society. Harvard and Yale awarded him LL.D. degrees, Harvard in 1945, at the Commencement just after the end of the war in Europe. The University of Hamburg followed in 1955, its gown including a starched white ruff that turned Langer into a living portrait by Holbein.

Langer's first marriage, in 1921, to Susanne Knauth, ended in divorce. In 1943 he married Rowena Morse Nelson. The Langers took adventurous trips abroad, played golf on two continents, shared in a love of literature, art, and good company, and enjoyed his arduous life of scholarship and public service as much as the holidays at Annisquam or overseas. For years he played the viola in quartets and was always a regular concertgoer. When illness struck him repeatedly in the 1970s, he fought back staunchly and resumed his work and his recreation as if there had been no interruption. Former students and younger colleagues found in him the most attentive of listeners and the kindest of advisers. He set a standard of excellence and probity that few could match; but lesser men found it stimulating to ask themselves from time to time if what they were saying or writing would meet with his approval and to hope that they were measuring up. This formidable man was paradoxically gentle, this realist and *Realpolitiker* was romantic and imaginative, this proud and self-made man with so much to be sure about was sometimes as uncertain and inse-cure—he says so himself—as the rest of us. His life and his achievement were from first to last a triumph and a fulfillment.

John K. Fairbank   Ernest R. May
Franklin L. Ford   Richard Pipes
Edward S. Mason   Robert Lee Wolff, *Chairman*

Memorial Minute
Faculty of Arts and Sciences
December 12, 1978

CHRONICLER OF THE HEROIC

"Historian of his university, state, navy and nation"

SAMUEL ELIOT MORISON

July 9, 1887 - May 15, 1976

Samuel Eliot Morison, the greatest American narrative historian since Francis Parkman, died in Boston, in his 89th year. He was then still living in the house at 44 Brimmer Street in which he had been born and which he had inherited from his grandfather, Samuel Eliot, who had built it in 1870. Such con-tinuities lie at the heart of Morison's career, shaped his achievement as a scholar and writer, and help explain his extraordinary service to Harvard College and University.

His contribution to the life of his alma mater fits no ordinary pattern. Except for one term at the University of California and three years at Oxford, he taught at Harvard all his professional life. But while his classes were always well regarded, they were never particularly popular, and he had very few graduate students. There is no "Morison school" of American historians, though many historians were influenced by him, and while he fulfilled his teaching obligations with his usual efficiency and style, he assumed no administrative duties of any kind and did not shape the development of historical studies in the university. Yet his contribution to the life of Harvard, like his contribution to the literature of history, was enormous and altogether unique. Peculiarly positioned to experience personally, as it were, the whole course of Harvard's history, he revealed it to the world and to itself as no one had ever done before and as no one will probably ever do again, and this was in miniature what he sought to do for his native state, for the life of those who sail the seas, and for the American nation.

Morison's family had been prominent in the history of Massachusetts and of Harvard almost from their founding, and the historian grew up at the very heart of proper Boston society. He recalled it in later years as an affluent but not extravagant community, provincial in some ways but wide in culture, tolerant, liberal, and devoted to reform causes. "It was never suggested," he wrote, "that 'Sammy' should go into business, or make money, or do anything but what his tastes and talents impelled him to do, no matter how unremunerative." As expected, he attended private schools in Boston, where he was taught a strictly classical curriculum, and then went off to St. Paul's School in New Hampshire, where the same kind of education was continued. By then he had long since become expert in the two sports that most interested him and that he continued to enjoy almost all his life: riding and sailing. He was as familiar with the many stables that then flourished in the Charles Street and Beacon Hill area as he was with the North Shore waters and the coast of Maine which he came to love above all other places on earth.

None of this was exceptional for a boy of his social position and physical vigor, nor was his entrance into Harvard with the Class of 1908. He fitted into college life easily, a handsome, vigorous, and affluent young man, and proceeded with no great distinction through a course of studies that emphasized mathematics, until suddenly, in his junior year, his academic interests took fire. It was then that he found in historical study the perfect field for his life work. He had been inspired in part by his teachers, whom he later described as the most distinguished group of historical scholars and teachers ever assembled on this continent; but the greatest influence was the writing of his grandfather's friend Francis Parkman. In Parkman's narrative volumes on the century of conflict between England and France in the New World, Morison found an inspiration that never faded. For Parkman was not only a capivating narrator but also "a man of the outdoors, an accomplished horseman, fisherman, and hunter, a lover of the great northern forest"; he wrote not as a library scholar but as a participant, visiting the scenes he described and living, for a time at least, as his subjects had lived. And yet Parkman had the self-discipline and thoroughness of the most devoted research scholar and the literary skill of a novelist.

It was that remarkable combination of scholarship, literature, and action all fused into the service of historical self-awareness that inspired the 24-year-old Morison and set the goals of his prodigiously productive life. A romantic? "No tags, please," Morison replied to this reiterated charge: "read me first!" But he *was* a romantic, from the moment his interest in history dawned. He cast everything he wrote into a dramatic structure of human struggle, and conveyed in every way he could the passion that he knew underlies human events. From the very beginning he thought of himself as a storyteller (history, he never tired of repeating, *had* to be a story: "Who will read Sir Lewis Namier tomorrow?") and the stories had to be involving and in some way heroic.

The fit of Morison's choice of career with his temperament and natural gifts was remarkable. Inspired by the romance of history, he nevertheless had extraordinary technical abilities. He was exceptionally self-disciplined, a good linguist, and capable of the most exacting and concentrated study of documents and the most prolonged efforts of composition. He had an instinct for accuracy of details and for unstrained common sense in interpretation, and an almost flawless ear for natural and effective

35

prose rhythms. Above all, he had the urge, indeed the passion, to express his personality in writing. He did not pick subjects defined by the objective progress of historical knowledge; he did not define problems systematically or attempt to resolve the strategic blockages in historical understanding. He proceeded as a poet, taking as subjects personal interests, things he loved and knew personally.

He began his professional career, after a year of study in Paris, with a doctoral dissertation on the life of his great-grandfather, Harrison Gray Otis, using family papers conveniently stored on Brimmer Street. Published in 1913, this solid two-volume "life and times" biography—rather charmless by Morison's standards but a distinguished piece of historical writing by normal criteria—established his professional reputation. In his second book, *The Maritime History of Massachusetts* (1921), he found direct expression for his love of the sea and was able to pour into it all the knowledge he had acquired of sailing the Atlantic waters and all the lore he had picked up from the old sailors whose memories went back to the days of the great clipper ships. It was his first work of art, written from start to finish in a single 11-month burst of energy, and it remains a wonderfully readable, informative book—and yet a very personal document.

By the time it appeared he was a lecturer in history at Harvard, having taught for a term at the University of California and having served briefly in the army and with the research team of the American delegation to the Versailles peace conference. In 1922 he was appointed the first Harmsworth Professor of American History at Oxford University, where he remained until 1925. While there, with his usual diligence, he completed an edition of documents of the American Revolution and the one-volume *Oxford History of the United States*, the forerunner of the immensely popular survey he published with Henry Steele Commager in 1930, *The Growth of the American Republic*. But the great events of the Oxford years took place not in England but in Spain, which he visited in 1925. In the Columbian Library in Seville he was shown Ferdinand Columbus's copy of the works of the tragedian Seneca, with the strange prophecy of the discovery of America, next to which Morison saw inscribed in Ferdinand's hand "'This prophecy was fulfilled by my father . . . the Admiral in the year 1492.'" At that moment, Morison later recalled, he determined to get on with the work on Columbus he had been contemplating, to follow his voyages personally by sail and so to get to the truth of the question of Columbus's own contribution to the epochal discovery.

On the same trip Morison was taken to the chapter house of the cathedral of Toledo, and there he saw the great series of portraits of the cardinal archibishops from the beginning of the Christian church to the present. "And when I looked at that, I said, how short our annals are in the United States. What would be the longest series of people I could find? Ah, I have it . . . the presidents of Harvard College, from 1636 on." With the Harvard Tercentenary only 11 years away, plans should be made to write the whole history of America's oldest institution, and Morison decided to do it. Upon his return to Harvard, now as full professor, he proposed to President Lowell that he be appointed Harvard's official historian on its 300th anniversary and be given full access to the archives and subsidies for the eventual publications. Lowell agreed, and Morison's first major project was launched. The books that resulted, published on schedule in 1936, were *The Founding of Harvard College*; the two-volume *Harvard College in the 17th Century*; the extraordinarily readable survey, *Three Centuries of Harvard*; and the edition of essays, *The Development of Harvard University, 1869-1929*. Of these five volumes, which together comprise the *Tercentennial History of Harvard College and University* the first three volumes, on the early years, form a masterpiece of historical writing. They not only elevated Harvard's history to a new plane of sophistication and completeness and celebrated the Puritans' commitment to learning in an unforgettable way, but revealed aspects of American cultural history until then unknown. The College and University could now be seen as national rather than regional institutions, consistent with President Conant's effort to broaden their constituencies to the nation at large.

Offshoots of this major effort appeared in characteristic profusion: *Builders of the Bay Colony* (1930), a volume of biographical studies of the Puritan leaders; *The Puritan Pronaos* (1935), an intellectual history of Puritan New England; and a string of monographic essays on technical problems he encountered in writing the Harvard histories. And during the same years Morison founded and largely edited *The New England Quarterly* a journal that still flourishes.

When the Harvard volumes were through the press Morison turned back to his other resolve of 1925, to write an exhaustive biography of Columbus based on a personal retracing of the discover's ocean voyages. Harvard friends and the College itself produced the funds and equipment he needed, and Morison launched the famous Harvard Columbus expedition. His two vessels roamed the ocean sea in 1939-40, following Columbus from Spain to the Canaries, then through the Caribbean islands and along the Spanish Main, verifying every reported landfall, checking every observation and journal entry. The resulting biography, *Admiral of the Ocean Sea* (1942), vindicated Columbus's claims and established him for the first time as a skilled navigator. The book, which proved to be extremely popular, also greatly magnified Morison's and Harvard's fame, brought the historian the first of two Pulitzer prizes, and paved the way for the easy acceptance by President Roosevelt and the United States Navy of Morison's next major project, his monumental *History of the United States Naval Operations in World War II.*

Like the Harvard history, the naval history was Morison's idea. Roosevelt, a Navy man whom Morison had known slightly, admired the Columbus book and welcomed Morison's proposal that he be appointed the nation's official historian of naval operations in World

War II. Here was the ultimate opportunity for all of Morison's ambitions, the perfect fusion of all his interests. He would participate personally, aboard any vessel he chose, in the greatest naval war in history, and he would have access to all the evidence, printed and oral, public and secret, that could be produced. Only Thucydides, among historians, had seen so great a struggle at such close hand and enjoyed the freedom afterwards to write the story out in full.

Morison was 55, recently appointed Jonathan Trumbull Professor of American History, when, as official historian with the rank of lieutenant commander, he joined his first naval operation; he was 75, retired from Harvard and from the Navy with the rank of rear admiral, when in 1962 he published the fifteenth and final volume of his naval history. It is a fabulous achievement. A participant's history, based on a veritable mountain of documentation, it attempts to portray the entire panoramic scene of battle on all oceans of the globe while depicting in finest detail exactly what happened in every engagement and why. The apparent ease with which Morison assembled this immense story, with the help of a very small staff of assistants and his faithful secretary, Antha Card, is almost miraculous. Even more remarkable is the unflagging drama of the narrative and its integrity as a single story.

The honors that fell to him when the dimensions of this accomplishment became clear surpass those accorded any modern historian. He was treated like royalty when he traveled abroad, and in his own country he had become an institution long before the United States Information Service recognized the fact in 1975 and filmed for the record and for foreign audiences the hour-long interview with him at his house in Northeast Harbor, Maine.

By then, the year before he died, he had long since put the naval history behind him and had completed the last of his major projects, which he had conceived in vague form while working out the Columbus book decades before. It was a comprehensive narrative of all the coastal explorations of North and South America, based on personal retracings, by sailing vessel and airplane, of the voyages of discovery which had revealed the boundaries of the New World. With the assistance of friends, Morison sailed and flew in the tracks of all the discoverers—verified their journals, mapped their landfalls and the ruins of their settlements, and boiled the whole massive story of their accomplishments into two big volumes crowded with maps, photographs, portraits, and charts, which he called *The European Discovery of America*. The first volume appeared in 1971, when Morison was 84; the second in 1974 two years before he died.

Morison's energy at every stage of this lifelong career of historical writing was prodigious, and he worked with apparent ease. Down to World War II he never wrote in the summers but spent those months sailing, traveling, and reading, and he advised young historians to do likewise. But as he grew older time became more precious to him, and as he wrote at the age of 76, "Knowing that death will break my pen I now work almost the year round, praying to be spared to write what is in me to write." In his last 30 years he turned out one small book almost every summer, while moving ahead on his major projects. The many works of these years are not all of uniformly high quality. The discipline that had controlled the personal expression in the Harvard series and the naval history began to slip. The writing became somewhat self-indulgent, the author's personality increasingly intrusive. But the books continued to charm and Morison's protean creativity remained unimpeded. A preliminary bibliography lists a total of well over 50 volumes, and no one knows how many journal articles, scholarly notes, speeches, and private publications he wrote.

And yet, for all of this, he remained an amateur rather than a professional historian much like his master, Parkman, though he had skills and knowledge that Parkman never dreamed of. He had no interest in keeping up with the latest developments in historical interpretation or technique, dismissing applied psychology and analytical, not to say quantitative, history as a betrayal of the historian's obligation to tell the human story of what had happened. Professional colleagues, even those who knew him well, found him an imposing but stiff, unbending, and rather taciturn personage. The story is told that once Morison attended the national historical convention, and to everyone's surprise, appeared on the hotel mezzanine, crowded with wheeling-dealing, gossiping academics. Into the melee he strode, tall, erect as always, his hands cocked in his jacket pockets, peering myopically ahead into the middle distance. The crowd fell silent and parted before him, and then, as he walked on, closed behind him at a respectful distance. And so, with his characteristic half-smile directed at one and all, he paced back and forth through the crowd, passing immaculate on dry land. Finally an old friend of his from Boston came on the scene, went up to Morison and said, "Sam, what are you doing?" "Doing?" said Morison with surprise. *"Doing!"* Why what do you think I'm doing? *Mixing!"*

To the post-war generation of students at Harvard he was a magisterial figure from a distant world. He insisted that the men in his classes wear coat and tie, and he himself lectured at times in naval uniform or in riding breeches. The latter was less surprising to those who recalled that when he started his teaching career as assistant to Albert Bushnell Hart he used to gallop over to Massachusetts Hall from Brimmer Street and pack up his bluebooks in saddle bags before continuing his ride. He seldom made specific appointments, suggesting to people who wanted to talk with him that they "just stop around some time" at his study in Widener Library. But when they did, they often found him preoccupied with his own work and forgetful even of who the visitors were. Yet he was not in fact either arrogant or snobbish. He was an utterly private man, sensitive in a most complex way, uneasy with people who were not part of his own social sphere, and removed from the everyday broils of academic life.

His remoteness from the ordinary scene was at times amusing. He recorded laconically in one autobiographical account that he had won what he called "the usual prizes given to historians." But in fact these usual prizes in his case included: two Pulitzer prizes, two Bancroft prizes, the Loubat Prize, the Jusserand Prize, the Christopher Award, the St. Thomas More Award, the Mahon Award, the Emerson-Thoreau Medal of the American Academy of Arts and Sciences, the gold medal of the American Academy of Arts and Letters, the Kennedy Medal of the Massachusetts Historical Society, the Presidential Medal of Freedom, seven battle stars of the U.S. Navy, the Legion of Merit with Combat Clasp, the Order of Merit of the Italian government with the rank of Commendatore, 12 honorary degrees, and the Balzan Foundation Award, which he and three others shared with the pope.

Morison cultivated his privacy. He gave instructions that no memorial service be held for him at Harvard and took steps to see to it that no one would write a personal biography of him. In the end it was a vulnerable sensibility that he was protecting; but it was always exposed. He could no more suppress his feelings than he could stop writing. He was deeply attached to his first wife, Elizabeth Greene, writing for private circulation a book in her memory when she died in 1945. For his second wife, Priscilla Barton, 19 years his junior, he displayed an affection bordering on adoration. To her he dedicated almost every book he wrote after their marriage in 1949, and when she died in 1973, he published privately a profoundly felt and moving memoir of her life and of their marriage. He had begun it in 1970 when he was 83, in the fear, he wrote, that he would die without leaving behind for her to read a testimony of his love, appreciation, and respect. Such sensibility was the deepest part of Morison's nature. It was the sensibility of an artist, but an artist who lived by a special credo, which he requested be inscribed on his gravestone: *"Dream dreams, then write them—aye, but live them first!"*

He was, in the Latin meaning of the word, superb: proud, bold, egregious; and he cast some of the spell of his imposing personality and of his ceaseless creativity over this College and University, for which he had a lifelong affection and which he served, in his unique way, for 40 years.

Paul H. Buck   Frederick Merk
Oscar Handlin   John H. Parry
                Bernard Bailyn, *Chairman*

Memorial Minute
Faculty of Arts and Sciences
May 3, 1977

AFRICANIST

"New ways of looking at African history"

KENNETH ONWUKA DIKE

December 17, 1917 - October 26, 1983

Kenneth Onwuka Dike, a renowned African scholar, educator, and statesman, led the way in revolutionizing African historiography. He was one of the first Africans trained as an historian who examined the history of Africa from the inside as it appeared in the written records and the remembrance of Africans, rather than entirely from the outside through the viewpoints of explorers, missionaries, businessmen, and colonial administrators. When the University of Michigan awarded him an honorary degree in 1979, the citation hailed him for bringing a shift in the field of African history, which like that of Copernicus in astronomy, caused us "to change our perceptions." In the 1970s Dike introduced his approach at Harvard where he served as the first Andrew W. Mellon Professor of African History and as chairman of the Committee on African Studies.

Both in his family history and in his own life, Dike epitomized the transformation of Africa in the twentieth century. His roots were in Awka [Oka], an Igbo [Ibo] community in present-day Nigeria, for generations

44

known for its skilled ironworkers. Changes began with his grandfather, Dike Nwanchọọ, a chief and trader, whose fleet of large canoes plied the Niger River, carrying on a trade that was to be the focal point of the younger Dike's historical studies. It was also significant that Dike Nwanchọọ in 1898 welcomed Anglican missionaries when they brought their religion and educational system to the town. At the same time he was the last person to have performed the responsibilities connected with the highest traditional title, Vum. In consequence, the grandson, Kenneth Dike, was trained for leadership both among his people and in the church and its educational system. His parents died when he was young, and his grandfather prepared him to be a potential successor as chief, signifying this intent by appointing the youth to carry to meetings the chief's symbol of power, a carved stool. But there was to be no successor as Vum.

An even greater influence was Dike's elder brother, George, a teacher in government schools, who brought him up and encouraged him to obtain an education. Young Kenneth was one of only 15 students from the Anglican diocese on the Niger admitted to the Dennis Memorial Grammar School, and in 1936 was one of the first graduates, the "glorious set," all of whom passed the senior Cambridge school certificate examination. His first university level training was at Fourah Bay College in Sierra Leone. At first he wished to become an Anglican priest, then shifted his focus to education, aspiring to return to the staff of the grammar school he had attended. His history professor, W. N. McMillan, author of *Complex South Africa: Bantu, Boer and Briton*, urged him toward higher goals. These became possible when Dike won a British Council scholarship to the University of Aberdeen. There he received first class honors in the M.A. examination, together with prizes, and a fellowship which took him on to the University of London and his doctor's degree. In Britain he studied under two outstanding colonial historians, Vincent Harlow and Gerald

S. Graham, Rhodes Professor of the British Empire (who as a young man had taught at Harvard).

African history was an uncertain new field that was not in high repute when Dike undertook his graduate studies. In 1967 from firsthand experience he wrote in the *Unesco Courier*:

> In Britain a few years ago, the authorities of the University of London were very sceptical when a degree course in African History was first mooted and waited until 1963 before establishing a Chair of African History. Perhaps in the academic world of today, Professor Trevor Roper of Oxford is not alone in his view that African History is no more than "the unrewarding gyrations of barbarous tribes in picturesque but irrelevant corners of the globe."

Dike was in the forefront of those who demonstrated that a new sort of African history could indeed be rewarding. He was fortunate enough to work for his doctorate at a time when both historians and anthropologists were going beyond the documents in the archives of the colonial powers and taking also into account the historical evidence and perspective of the African peoples. Dike's dissertation, completed in 1949, appeared with revision in 1956 as the monograph, *Trade and Politics in the Niger Delta, 1830-85*. It is an application of scholarly historical research and analysis to the Nigerian traders in palm oil sought after by Merseyside soap manufacturers. These traders for some decades served successfully as middlemen between the African producers and the British purchasers. The most successful among them, an Igbo named Jaja, ruled one of several city-states along the coast. Gradually the British exercised more direct influence, finally in the 1880s establishing a protectorate. Soon their steam launches began to supplant the giant canoes on the Niger. As the Africanist J. D. Fage writes, Dike's study "'is usually considered the first fruit of the new university-based approach to the history of Africa."

When Dike completed his doctoral studies, West African nations were moving toward independence and national universities were coming into being. In 1950 he joined the faculty of the emerging university at Ibadan, Nigeria. There in the next few years he became the first professor of history and created a program for interdisciplinary research into Nigerian history, the Benin history research scheme, which became a model throughout Sub-Saharan Africa. There too he became closely associated with a notable historian of the age of expansion, John H. Parry, whom he succeeded as principal of the University College. In 1962 Dike became the first vice chancellor of the University of Ibadan—"a fate which seems all too commonly to befall African historians," Fage notes, "perhaps because departments of history in African universities are among the first to become Africanized."

As an historian, Dike was in the forefront in demonstrating that Africans possessed a past in which they could take pride. Through founding the National Archives of Nigeria and a number of related activities, he helped preserve records, a few of which in Arabic went back to the tenth century. In addition, since there was a dearth of documentary evidence, he fostered oral history, comparative linguistics, and archeology. He created and headed the Institute of African Studies at the University of Ibadan and was chairman of the International Congress of Africanists when it held its first meeting at Accra, Ghana under the sponsorship of Unesco. He became the scientific director of the Unesco project for a general history of Africa. As that project was taking shape, he declared:

> There is now no need to belabor that Africa has a history worthy of study at all levels of intellectual discipline. More than that, it is now generally accepted that the history of Africa must be the history of the African peoples themselves—that their actions, not the actions of the invaders, must be the focus of African history.

Above all, Dike achieved his remarkable standing because of his position as head of University College, Ibadan (and the full university that followed). It was one of only five universities in anglophonic Africa prior to 1965. Thus Dike presided over a major center of higher education in the Sub-Saharan region, which had few others. During Dike's stewardship, Ibadan had an exciting intellectual atmosphere, with Nigerians and foreigners working together in the arts, medicine, agriculture and the social sciences. They accomplished much imporant research and trained the first sizable generation of Nigerian scholars and scientists. Many of these people went abroad to complete their studies and returned to become leaders in Nigeria. They revered Dike as a pioneer in the development of their country. He played a unique role in Nigerian, indeed in African, history by being the first in so many accomplishments; education-conscious Nigerians in the 1980s view him as a legendary figure despite his role in the Biafran movement.

Although Dike had contributed enormously to the development of historical studies and higher education in Nigeria, he felt he must side with the Igbos in the eastern part of the country from which he had come when they sought to secede in the late 1960s. During the ensuing civil war, he served the Republic of Biafra as ambassador-at-large. With the collapse of the Biafran cause in 1970, he accepted a professorship at Harvard, where his former colleague Parry had become Gardiner Professor of Oceanic History.

For a decade Dike nurtured an African program at Harvard and was active in the history department and the university. What meant most to Dike was keeping an African presence alive and visible at Harvard: the African seminar (which Rupert Emerson had originated), the Committee on African Studies which promoted and coordinated curricular and extracurricular activities relating to Africa, and just before he left, a course on African civilization in the core curriculum. His enormous concern that the new Harvard program have a course on Africa from its inception represents at its best his interest in promoting African studies at Harvard. He was dismayed that Harvard had given a collection of African publications to the Boston University Library sometime before his arrival, and he constantly campaigned to extend African acquisitions in the library. He was interested also in Americans of African origins. He participated in the establishment of the W. E. B. Du Bois Research Institute in Afro-American Studies and served on the search committee for members of the newly established Afro-American Studies Department.

Throughout the United States Dike's counsel was sought on many matters, particularly in African studies but sometimes as far removed as the selection of fellows for the newly created National Center for the Humanities in North Carolina. He was recipient of numerous honors; altogether he received 15 honorary degrees.

Scholarly life was engrossing to Dike. He spent much time in Widener Library, and in his study at home among his large collection of books, preparing public lectures and working upon a monograph on "The Aro and Their Neighbors: A Study of the African Middleman of the Hinterland Slave Trade in Eastern Nigeria from the Seventeenth to the Eighteenth Century."

Nevertheless, Dike was troubled because he sensed that African studies did not hold a high priority at Harvard. In a sense he was back at the beginning of his career when African history had to justify itself as a legitimate field of inquiry. There had been a great upsurge in African studies in the United States during the 1960s, but its major centers were elsewhere.

Further, the tug of Nigeria was strong. From the time Dike was a youth, one of his fervent aspirations had been to be of help to his people. When he was 21 he wrote in his diary:

> True leadership is service . . . Africa cannot rise unless her sons learn how to lead rightly. Most of our men after their university careers use their learning to exploit their fellow-Africans . . . Oh the pity of it! Countrymen,

arise; let us work together, throw off pride and arrogance and put on aprons of service!

In 1980 he decided to retire early, putting behind him his position at Harvard in order to return to service in Nigeria. He undertook to establish what was projected as a chain of regional technical institutes. At the time of his death, he was president of the first of these, the Anambra State University of Technology. He was mourned in Nigeria as a national hero; educational institutions throughout the country closed in his memory. During his career he had always worn his apron of service.

Oscar Handlin   Robert A. LeVine
Martin L. Kilson   Preston N. Williams
                    Frank Freidel, *Chairman*

Memorial Minute
Faculty of Arts and Sciences
May 20, 1986

MEDIEVAL HISTORIAN

"Something of a Cam cult among undergraduates"

HELEN MAUD CAM

August 22, 1885 - February 9, 1968

Helen Maud Cam came to Harvard University in 1948 as the first holder of the Zemurray Radcliffe Professorship. A distinguished career in England already lay behind her. Born in 1885, one of nine children of the Reverend William Herbert Cam and his wife Kate, she was educated at home by her parents, whom she called in the dedication of one of her books "my first and best teachers." Disappointed in her hopes of following in her father's footsteps at Oxford, she took her B.A. degree in 1907 at Royal Holloway College, in the University of London, and spent the following year as fellow in history at Bryn Mawr. There she not only laid the foundation of her lifelong affection for the United States but also wrote much of her M.A. thesis on *Local Government in Francia and England*, which was published by the University of London in 1912. Following a decade as lecturer on history at Royal Holloway College, she moved in 1922 to Cambridge, where she served successively as research fellow and lecturer at Girton College and as University lecturer on history from 1927 until 1948. From 1944, she was also vice-mistress of Girton. During these years a steady flow of books and articles came from her pen, dealing mostly with the history of local government and representative assemblies in England, and her scholarly distinction was recognized by numerous academic honors, including a LITT.D. from Cambridge, a fellowship in the British Academy, and a vice-presidency of the Royal Historical Society.

She came to Harvard, therefore, as a well-known historian, and at an age when most scholars are looking forward to retirement rather than launching out on a new career. Many of those who remember her find it hard to believe that she was here only six years. Students from many fields were attracted to her lectures not only by her mastery of her subject-matter but also by the enthusiasm with which she tackled even the most recondite historical problems. There was something of a "Cam cult" among undergraduates, and the *Crimson* in a profile written shortly before her retirement said that her "intense activity and interest have helped close a wide gap of age and culture." Though the last person to think of herself as a pioneer, she established many significant precedents as first woman professor in the Faculty of Arts and Sciences, including her use of Lamont Library and attendance at morning chapel. In every respect she gave herself freely to Harvard and to Radcliffe, and to the academic community in this country. Yet she found time to continue her scholarly research and writing, and she received several honorary degrees and memberships.

Her years at Harvard meant more to Miss Cam, however, than the natural satisfaction she felt in these activities and distinctions. They did much to broaden her perspectives and change her style of life after 25 years in a Cambridge college, and she was older only in years when she returned to England upon her retirement in 1954. In her home at Sevenoaks, where she lived with her sister Norah, she continued to work with undiminished vigor almost until the day of her death, and her friends who visited her there will long remember her beloved garden and tiny study, packed with books, where she worked on her edition of the 1321 eyre of London. She remained an active member of various learned societies and frequently attended historical conferences both in England and abroad. She made her last visit to this country in 1967, when she saw many old friends, and made new ones, at Harvard. In 1957 she was awarded a c.b.e. and in 1962 an honorary litt.d. from Oxford. Her international eminence in the historical profession was recognized by the publication in 1960-61 of two volumes of essays written in her honor by 36 scholars from 13 different countries.

Helen Cam was far more than a distinguished historian, however, as her friends and colleagues knew. She brought to every sphere of her life the same passionate concern for accuracy and honesty with which she studied medieval history. Her work and mind were marked by energy and common sense rather than subtlety, but her creative sensitivity showed in her water-colors and drawings (as recipients of her Christmas cards will remember) and in her love of literature, especially historical novels, upon which she was a recognized authority—though woe betide the writer who took liberties with historical accuracy! She loved a well-informed discussion and was outspoken in private conversation, as in historical debate; but no one who saw her dozing in her chair after dinner, or laughing heartily at one of her own absent-minded foibles, could regard her as formidable. Behind her impressive learning and forthright manner lay a warm, loyal, and generous nature, equally incapable of giving or taking offense.

A strong sense of personal engagement and responsibility inspired Miss Cam's life and carried her into a wide range of activities. She was a strong supporter of the Labor Party in England and worked for a number of educational and youth organizations. She took a special interest after her retirement in Hillcroft College, for women who have been deprived of educational opportunities at the normal time. These commitments were an expression of her religious convictions, founded in her enlightened Victorian upbringing. "We must not keep our religion and our work in two watertight compartments," she said in her chapel talk of 1953. "Our God is not as small as that. His kingdom and His righteousness must come first; we must seek Him in our academic studies, confident that all work well done is work done for the advancement of His purposes, and that all knowledge of the world He created can be a means of enlarging our knowledge of Him."

Wilbur K. Jordan   Samuel E. Thorne
Giles Constable, *Chairman*

Memorial Minute
Faculty of Arts and Sciences
November 12, 1968

POLITICAL THEORIST

"He appeared to have read everything"

CHARLES HOWARD McILWAIN

March 15, 1871 - June 1, 1968

Born in Saltsburg, Pennsylvania, Charles Howard McIlwain graduated from the College of New Jersey, later Princeton University, in 1894, and after reading law in a Pittsburgh law office, was admitted to the Pennsylvania Bar in 1897. He fortunately did not choose to follow the law, though he always retained a keen interest in it, particularly in its history, but returned instead to Princeton, proceeding to an M.A. in 1898. He removed to Cambridge sometime before 1903, for in that year he received a Harvard A.M. He taught at Miami University in Ohio from 1903 to 1905, then at Princeton, as one of President Wilson's original group of preceptors. There he remained for five years, until 1910, when his path-breaking book, *The High Court of Parliament*, rejected by the Harvard University Press, was published by Yale and at once established his reputation. He had by then moved to Bowdoin College, as professor of history and government, but left it in 1911 for an assistant professorship in the same two subjects at Harvard. He had just been awarded a Harvard PH.D.

McIlwain was thus 40 years old when he began to teach History 9—the constitutional history of England— succeeding the eminent Charles Gross, his teacher and mentor, and in the Department of Government, a course on Roman law, its history and influence. He did not come to Government 6, a course with which he then became completely identified, until 1920. First introduced by Harold Laski, who was very proud of his successor, it reflected McIlwain's special interest in medieval political thought, and for many years had no counterpart in any other American university. He continued to teach these two related and justly famous courses until he retired at 75 from the Eaton Professorship.

McIlwain wrote five books, the most notable of which, besides *The High Court of Parliament*, were *The American Revolution*, which was awarded a Pulitzer Prize, and *The Growth of Political Thought in the West*. He ought to have published more, for his knowledge of the large and formidable literature of political theory was unrivaled, but he was excessively careful and loath to let his work leave his hands. He also edited four seventeenth-century texts, including a large quarto of political works of James I, and contributed more than 30 papers to historical and other journals, as well as to volumes of essays.

He was a member of a number of learned societies, among them the American Philosophical Society, a fellow of the Mediaeval Academy of America, a corresponding fellow of the British Academy. President of the American Historical Association in 1935-1936, he was Eastman Professor at Oxford in 1944. Honorary degrees were conferred upon him by many universities, among them Harvard, Yale, Princeton, and Chicago.

This bare recital, however, hardly does him justice. He was a scholar steeped in the thought of the past, through long acquaintance with its writings and records. To his students he appeared to have read everything, and to have kept it all vividly in mind. Indeed, he seemed to come to class fresh from conversations with Selden or Coke, Lambarde or Hooker, having just left them on the steps of Harvard Hall. They were his close friends, whose eloquent words, in books or parliamentary debate, were recalled with admiration and affection; it was otherwise on the days he walked to class with Rousseau, or with James I or Thomas Hobbes. So infectious was his enthusiasm, so evident his delight in the matter he expounded, that students, caught up in the great struggle between Boniface VIII and Philip the Fair, found themselves calling out of the bowels of Widener books which had not seen the light of day for a century. It was not by formal lectures that their interest was aroused, for McIlwain, at least in his later years, dealt with his subject by first reading a text, often a Latin text, and then explaining and illustrating it by a running commentary, drawn from an immense literature, with the whole of which his audience was flatteringly assumed to be completely familiar. It was hardly an orthodox method of instruction, but in his hands a most effective one.

The learning he expected his hearers to have was then often acquired, just as the interest he assumed them to have, if at first simulated, then became real. The group that gathered about his desk after the hour seldom disbanded before another had passed, and he was usually accompanied across the Yard by some not yet ready to end the discussion. Of course Egidius Romanus and Augustinus Triumphus did not appeal to everyone; there were some, even then, who found the Provisions of Oxford or the *Libelli de Lite* irrelevant. But all came away impressed by a vigorous intelligence, passionately interested in ideas; by a man of evident principle and transparent honesty; by a scholar of great eminence who was the most modest and unassuming of men.

McIlwain did not himself believe that what he taught was of purely historical and academic interest. He was horrified, as so many were, by what he saw happening in Europe in the 1930s, as rights were swept away and individuals found themselves helpless in the grasp of despotic governments. As an historian familiar with the erosion of liberties and the growth of despotisms, he recognized the appearance at home of some of the characteristic symptoms. Aware of how little it took to disturb the delicate balance between *gubernaculum* and *jurisdictio*, he spoke out strongly for a government limited by law. He was especially troubled by the plan for packing the Supreme Court, by proposed constitutional amendments limiting its power to review executive and legislative action, and by measures, then being considered, for the easy removal of judges. In articles in periodicals very different from those in which his writings had theretofore appeared, he denounced arbitrary governmental action and any curtailment of the rights and privileges on which an individualistic society and a humane civilization depend. He here added his own name to the long list of those who had fought for constitutionalism.

McIlwain was devoted to his graduate students and they to him. He was always ready to listen to their difficulties and to give whatever help he could. At professional meetings he was usually to be found surrounded by them, he as anxious to hear of their accomplishments as they were to tell him of them. For many years after his retirement, until he could no longer come to them, his former graduate students, some of them near their own retirements, celebrated his birthday with him, at a dinner given in his honor in Cambridge or elsewhere. At these annual events a toast was always drunk to a distinguished scholar, a stimulating and sympathetic teacher, and a genuine, kindly and warm-hearted friend. He invariably protested that the tribute was undeserved, but those who knew and worked with him had no such doubts. A simple statement of fact, no more and no less than his due.

Samuel H. Beer   Carl J. Friedrich
John P. Dawson   Myron P. Gilmore
                Samuel E. Thorne, *Chairman*

Memorial Minute
Faculty of Arts and Sciences
May 20, 1969

BIBLICAL SCHOLAR

"A new school of archeology"
GEORGE ERNEST WRIGHT
September 5, 1909 - August 29, 1974

George Ernest Wright, Parkman Professor of Divinity and Curator of the Harvard Semitic Museum, died of heart disease shortly after his return from an extended trip to the Near East. He was born in a Presbyterian manse in Zanesville, Ohio, and received his early academic training at the College of Wooster, Ohio,  and at the McCormick Theological Seminary in Chicago. Upon completion of his theological degree in 1934, he was ordained to the Presbyterian ministry. During his theological studies he came under the influence of Ovid R. Sellers, a biblical scholar with primary interests in Palestinian archeology. Sellers urged Wright to undertake a scholarly career and directed him to Johns Hopkins University to study with the distinguished Orientalist, William Foxwell Albright. At Johns Hopkins, Wright studied Semitic philology and ancient Near Eastern history. However, his chief interest and energies were increasingly focused on Syro-Palestinian archeology, and his doctoral dissertation dealt with the *Pottery of Palestine from Earliest Times to the End of the Early Bronze Age*. Its publication in 1937 immediately established his reputation as a ceramic typologist. Writing 30 years later, Ruth Amiran remarks in her standard work on Palestinian pottery that "Wright's books on the early periods . . . brought order into the early ceramic history of Palestine. . . . Most of [his] views are still valid despite the passage of time and the discoveries made since the book was published."

In 1938, Wright was appointed field secretary of the American Schools of Oriental Research in Jerusalem and Baghdad. However, Arab uprising and the Second World War following one upon another halted archeological excavation in Palestine and brought an end to Wright's first period of research in field archeology.

In 1939 Wright returned to McCormick Theological Seminary where he taught biblical languages and Old Testament literature and religion until he came to Harvard in 1958 as Parkman Professor of Divinity.

The Calvinist or Reformed tradition ran deep in Ernest Wright. Some will see his preoccupation with the Hebrew Scriptures as stemming from his Calvinism. In his inaugural address at McCormick, the Reformed theologian is most visible. He spoke to those in the Church who would drop the Old Testament from the Christian canon, or give it status inferior to that of the New Testament. The Old Testament, he argued, was the "bulwark of the Christian faith" against the antinomianism of much of Protestant Christianity, against perfectionist irresponsibility in politics, against the anti-Semitism that stains all of Christian history; in short, a bulwark against most of the heresies he found in modern Christianity. His most influential theological work is entitled *God Who Acts: Biblical Theology as Recital*, published in 1952. In it, he contended that biblical language and symbols were drawn from Israel's singular historical consciousness, and with the loss of such language, lost also was the understanding of human nature and destiny as historical, communal, political. Wright strove to bring to theological reflection the worldliness and "dynamism of the prophetic presence in Israel," as Noel Freedman has written, and while it has

60

become clear over the past quarter-century "that Wright's thesis was overstated . . . it has become clear because the dead hand of propositional and systematic dogmatics has been loosened from the neck of biblical studies, in no small part resulting from Wright's efforts."

To these same themes he returned in his last work in biblical theology, *The Old Testament and Theology*, published in 1969. At its conclusion, he quotes Whitehead with satisfaction: "religions commit suicide when they find their inspiration in dogmas. The inspiration of religion lies in the history of religion."

Ernest Wright's sense of vocation and work was certainly Calvinistic. He was author or co-author of a score of books and monographs. He suffered his first heart attack in 1957, but, in the next 16 years, his years at Harvard, he mounted expedition after expedition without break, to biblical Shechem, to Gezer, and in his last years to Idalion.

Ernest Wright is best known as an archeological scholar, and his contributions to Near Eastern archeology remain his most imposing and enduring scholarly monument. His expeditions and those of his students focused chiefly on Syro-Palestinian sites, but he dug also in Cyprus and at the time of his death was organizing an expedition to Carthage. Through the years, he has sent out from the Semitic Museum a steady stream of finely-trained specialists in the pottery of the eastern Mediterranean. His return to field archeology at Shechem gave him the opportunity to develop and test new methods of digging. His own training had been in techniques used by Albright, taken up and developed by Israeli archeologists, in which pottery typology was the chief chronological control. Meanwhile, the British had introduced new modes of stratigraphic control into Palestinian archeology borrowed from their experience in excavating Roman England. Wright proposed to combine the strengths of both methods, one in use largely in Arab lands, the other in Israel. Moreover, he turned his expeditions into training and testing grounds for young scholars to an unheard-of degree, abandoning the usual style in which the director of excavations is the great man who jealously guards the major results of his dig and claims all scholarly glory. Wright's audaciously eclectic methods brought into being a new school of Near Eastern archeologists which organized and directed the main thrust of American archeological research in the Near East in the last decade, a period roughly coinciding with his term as a uniquely vigorous president of the American Schools of Oriental Research. One happy and comforting result of his generous nurturing of young scholars is that, despite his death, his expeditions will continue without faltering, and the publication of his excavations will continue to completion.

Many remember Ernest Wright as a great teacher, and the picture comes to mind of him leaving the classroom—on an ordinary day during term—with his students standing and applauding. He was not a polished speaker. Yet he had an extraordinary power to persuade and to excite enthusiasm in the classroom. One of the marks of his teaching—and of his writing for that matter—was its clarity and honesty. He spoke with a Mid-western plainness of speech, and was less afraid of being wrong, or of appearing the fool, than of being obscure.

Since his death, two memorial volumes of essays have been published. One is entitled simply *Essays in Honor of George Ernest Wright*, prepared by his students. The second, a volume designed to be presented to him by his colleagues on his sixty-fifth birthday, bears the name *Magnalia Dei*, recalling a persistent theme in G. Ernest Wright's teaching and writing as it echoed his Calvinist forebears of early New England.

Paul D. Hanson   Krister Stendahl
William L. Moran   Frank Moore Cross, *Chairman*

Memorial Minute
Faculty of Divinity
March 18, 1977

III. Learning and Life

PRESIDENT

"A legacy of integrity, originality, courage"
JAMES BRYANT CONANT
March 26, 1893 - February 11, 1978

James Bryant Conant, eminent American chemist, innovative president of Harvard University, leader of the U.S. technological effort in the Second World War, postwar statesman of science, Ambassador to Germany, and controversial school reformer, died in Hanover, New Hampshire, at the age of 84.  To a considerable degree, Harvard today reflects the principles and practices that he instituted during the 20 years of his presidency.

Like President Eliot before him, Conant was a chemist and, like Eliot, he emphasized research and scholarship. He began at Harvard as a student of chemistry and continued, except for an interruption during World War I, on its chemistry staff. At a time when most American chemistry was decidedly second-rate by European standards, he won international recognition; his highly original contributions to physical-organic chemistry and to natural products chemistry have since been developed with great effect by others. Those fortunate enough to have carried out research under his direction remember him for his bold scientific imagination, for his incisive and critical judgment, and for his restraint when faced with the shortcomings of his students. In the spring of 1933, when Conant was appointed to succeed Lowell as president, his administrative experience was largely based on a term as chairman of the chemistry department.

He began his creative career as an activist president almost immediately after his appointment. In 1933, Harvard had no compulsory retirement age. Conant proposed one, and the Fellows adopted it, but a problem remained with respect to those senior professors who were already on the staff. Audaciously, he suggested that they retire at 76 and was gratified and relieved when Professor George Lyman Kittredge set a precedent by announcing that, at 76, he was retiring voluntarily. It remains to be seen whether, today, action of that kind will come to be regarded by the Congress as an unreasonable infringement on the right to work. Although Conant was spared a fight over that issue, his struggles with the faculty began soon enough.

Undergraduate Houses and the tutorial system of instruction had been introduced by President Lowell shortly after the First World War. The tutoring was done principally by younger faculty who, even had they all been excellent, were far too numerous to permit their wholesale promotion. Conant, spurred by the financial stringencies of the Great Depression, faced the unenviable task of communicating to departments the necessity of reducing these numbers. In March 1937, the University decided against the promotion of Raymond Walsh and Alan Sweezy, two popular instructors of economics who were also officers of the newly formed teachers union. Many of the faculty were outraged, and the case became something of a cause célèbre. Faculty meetings were stormy, to say the least, and at one point, to avoid what would have been in essence a vote of censure, Conant felt obliged to apologize for his failure to inform the faculty of the rules for tenure he was following. A group of professors, in response to a petition from more than a hundred of their colleagues, asked that they be appointed to review the case, and Conant had no choice but to comply. The group, which became known as the Committee of Eight, exonerated the University from charges of bias, but went on to recommend a set of criteria for promotion and tenure that established Harvard's eight-year "up or out" rule.

That rule, when finally adopted, kept the size of the faculty within bounds but did not assure its quality. In an imaginative measure designed to provide an institutional framework for achieving quality, Conant introduced the present system of ad hoc committees to evaluate proposed tenure appointments; this proved the single most important innovation of his presidency. Needless to say, Harvard had had many distinguished faculty prior to his administration; these included a Nobel laureate in chemistry, Theodore William Richards, whose daughter, Grace Richards, married Conant in 1921 and cherished and supported him throughout his demanding life. But at least in the sciences, full parity with our European colleagues came after, and in part because of, the ad hoc system. By chairing the meetings of the ad hoc committees, Conant established a tradition that our presidents can welcome as providing the best possible guarantee of excellence in the faculty, and that the faculty can welcome as providing the best possible education for our presidents.

Conant introduced much else. He instituted a system of national scholarships to attract brilliant students from all parts of the country without regard for their financial status. The search for the national scholars broadened the outlook of the admissions office, so that Harvard became unmistakably a national, rather than a New England institution. He similarly introduced the concepts of University professorships; the holders were to be independent of departmental responsibilities and were to engage in interdisciplinary teaching and research. In response to a bequest provided "to elevate the standards of journalism . . . ," he invented the Nieman fellowships; the arrangement has proved remarkably successful, and side-

67

stepped establishing a school of journalism. After the war, he initiated the Committee on General Education, to create for Harvard students a common educational experience based on the appreciation of the intellectual freedoms that had so recently been at risk.

Subsequently, Conant directed more and more of his attention to the University as a whole, rather than primarily to the Faculty of Arts and Sciences. He decentralized his administration and relied heavily on the "rugged deans" of the medical, law, business, and other schools. At the same time, he made a practice of chairing faculty meetings at the professional schools when appointments were discussed, so that he could more effectively interpret faculty recommendations to the governing boards; when other matters were debated, his quick analytical intelligence served to bring to bear relevant experience from other parts of the university. Conant also initiated the series of moves that have now resulted in the almost complete integration of Harvard and Radcliffe. This reform can be ascribed to his pragmatism and lack of prejudice rather than to ardent feminism—the idea of repeating lectures specifically for a Radcliffe audience offended his sense of thrift—but the achievement stands, and the initial move was his.

He later drew upon his wartime experience, where the national government had found basic science of the greatest practical importance, to transform Harvard's School of Engineering into a division of the Faculty of Arts and Sciences; he drew upon his familiarity with federal secrecy procedures to establish the rule that Harvard would not in peacetime accept classified research projects. During the years when he participated extensively in the federal government, he leaned heavily on Paul Buck, dean of the Faculty of Arts and Sciences and later provost of the university, whose diplomatic and administrative skills admirably complemented his own.

Although his accomplishments in remaking Harvard are paramount, something must be said of his other careers. Conant, like many of the leading American chemists of his day, had studied for a while in Germany; he returned home with an appreciation of German science and an apprehension of German militarism. At the outbreak of the Second World War, he became desperately concerned with the dangers that the Nazis posed for the United States and, while president of Harvard, spoke out vigorously on the subject. His views were as controversial as his administrative reforms had been a few years earlier. Subsequently, as chairman of the National Defense Research Committee, he carried the major responsibility for the technical direction of war research. After the war, he turned down the invitation to become the first chairman of the Atomic Energy Commission, but accepted the chairmanship of the National Science Board, where he established the policies that set the direction of the National Science Foundation. During the McCarthy era, he went on record with a vigorous public defense of Robert Oppenheimer. From 1953 to 1955, after he had resigned the presidency of Harvard, he served with distinction as U.S. high commissioner, and then as ambassador, to Germany. He was widely regarded throughout the Federal Republic as a scientist who valued German scholarship and was appreciated especially for his help in rebuilding German cultural institutions. In all of his governmental roles Conant performed admirably, with the crispness and, when required, with the asperity that were his hallmarks. In particular, as co-chairman of the military policy committee of the Manhattan District, he enraged a number of scientists—mostly chemists—by opposing some of the procedures they advocated for creating the atomic bomb. In the event, his judgments proved sound, and the work went forward with what, in retrospect, can only be considered miraculous speed.

In his later years Conant undertook a massive study of secondary schools; his books on the subject (*The American High School Today*, *The Citadel of Learning*, and others) focused on the importance to America of the public high schools. In 1961, well ahead of the widespread unrest that surfaced later in that decade, he warned, in his *Slums and Suburbs*, of the social dynamite inherent in the growing numbers of unemployed urban youths.

For all his prominence, he felt no self-importance, treated people as equals, and talked with them frankly and lucidly, sometimes with sparkling humor or, though he was not an emotional man, with sudden sympathy. He judged others as firmly as he judged himself but, once confident of them, gave them his full loyalty, which they reciprocated. His manner toward the young was refreshingly unassuming; on visiting the Houses, he would find interesting undergraduates and talk with them as attentively as with any professor—more eagerly, perhaps, as if their directness resembled his. Straightforward, reserved yet outspoken, meticulously fair, self-confident enough to be self-critical, given to thoughtful decisions and precise rather than brilliant language, he was less a modern New Englander than a descendant of the Puritans, and he held himself as accountable as they.

During the Senate hearings on his confirmation as U.S. high commissioner for Germany, he was as outspoken as ever. His college classmate, Senator Leverett Saltonstall, explained that Harvard expects its presidents to be controversial figures, whereupon Senator Homer Ferguson remarked to Conant that ". . . there seems no doubt they got one when they got you." But institutional change can seldom be effected without controversy. America, science, and particularly Harvard, are the beneficiaries of Conant's willingness to face problems with integrity, originality, and courage; the strength of our University today bears witness to his success.

Paul H. Buck	George B. Kistiakowsky
John H. Finley	Edward S. Mason
Paul A. Freund	Don K. Price

Frank H. Westheimer, *Chairman*

Memorial Minute
Faculty of Arts and Sciences
November 14, 1978

HISTORIAN

"An extraordinary human being"
DAVID OWEN
December 2, 1898 - February 13, 1968

David Owen was born in Owatonna, Minnesota. He received his early education at Pillsbury Academy, where his father was a member of the faculty, and at Denison University in Granville, Ohio, where he graduated in 1922.

When in 1922 he arrived at Yale to begin graduate work, his chosen field was Chinese history. The titles of his first publications after he had received his PH.D. in 1927— *Imperialism and Nationalism in the Far East* (1929) and *British Opium Policy in China and India* (1934)—indicate that he retained his interest in that part of the world for some time. But by the time the second of these books appeared—he was by then an assistant professor of history at Yale—he had, to quote his own later account, "sort of backed into" English history. It turned out to be a fortunate collision of which Harvard was the chief beneficiary.

In 1937 David Owen came to Cambridge from New Haven as a one-year visitor. He stayed for the rest of his life, becoming an associate professor in 1938, a full professor in 1946, and Gurney Professor of History and

Political Science in 1958. In the course of this period he established himself as an indispensable member of this faculty in a variety of ways: as a teacher and scholar; as an administrator; and, above all, as a human being.

His most famous course was History 142b, the history of England in the nineteenth century. Even the most jaded and indifferent undergraduates could not help but become caught up in the six points of the Charter and the plight of the ten-pound householder, when these matters were put before them with the energy and vividness that were David Owen's trademark. It was in this course that he delivered his famous "Crystal Palace" lecture on the Great Exhibition of 1851 which he himself— in his customary self-deprecatory manner—came to regard as "a parlor trick," but which will be remembered by thousands as a brilliant recreation of the spirit of an age. Needless to say, History 142b was a perpetual favorite of the *Confidential Guide* which even went so far as explicitly to forgive the lecturer some of his more outrageous puns. Harvard undergraduates admired and respected David Owen not only as a vivid and dramatic lecturer but also as someone who treated them as whole persons, without the slightest pomp or condescension. They relished his description of themselves as "not a particularly docile lot, but reasonable when backed into a corner"; and, just because he never patronized them, did not resent his occasionally making fun of them. "None of us is infallible, not even the very young," he remarked not so long before his death.

But if undergraduates admired David Owen, his graduate students were devoted to him. Not only did he hold out high standards for them in his seminars, but his concern for each and every one of them was legendary. He encouraged them, he got them jobs, he knew and sympathized with their problems and frustrations. He never forgot a face, or a first name; and has been aptly described as the only member of the Harvard faculty who actually *enjoyed* office hours. During his many years as chairman of the Department of History his forthrightness, his wit, and his warmth gained for him the trust and affection not only of his colleagues and his own students, but also of all who came in contact with him. For those who believe in the elective affinities that draw together the historian and his subject, it should have come as no surprise that his major historical work was to be concerned with the history of charity. After all, one of the definitions of that virtue—dating back to the fifteenth century—is "a disposition to judge hopefully of men and their actions, and to make allowance for their shortcomings."

David Owen's *English Philanthropy, 1660-1960* appeared in 1964. In taking on this assignment, he had set himself as ambitious a theme as any historian of the period has ever tackled, no less than the history of the transition from voluntary charitable effort in the seventeenth and eighteenth centuries to the triumph of the welfare state in our own century. The book is a storehouse of learning, beautifully organized, and presented clearly and cogently; and will remain the standard work on the subject for some time to come.

One of the amazing things about this book is that David Owen found time to write it at all. The chairmanship of the history department was only one of the many administrative tasks he took on during his years at Harvard. During World War II he was for some years assistant to the dean of the faculty. From 1949 to 1952 he served as chairman of the Committee on General Education; and from 1957 to 1964 as master of Winthrop House, where the same qualities that had made him one of Harvard's great teachers made him both a popular and a respected master. He was a senior fellow of the Society of Fellows from 1964 until his death, at which time he was also a member of several standing and special committees, including one of his favorites, the Faculty Committee on Athletic Sports. Any committee on which he sat benefited from his fairness, his patience, and—not least—his ready wit.

But above all, David Owen will be remembered as an extraordinary human being. Those who knew him well also knew that the sardonic exuberance of the lecture platform formed but a small part of a sensitive and complex personality. Thus, he had an almost uncannily sharp ear for the false quantities of human discourse. No one was ever more allergic to the obvious and the second-rate. Yet this allergy to the mediocre went along not with any sort of mandarin aloofness; but, rather, with a fundamental attitude of amused benevolence toward his fellow men. It is also true that David Owen could not abide even the slightest hint of the maudlin and the sentimental. Thus, he always left a meeting or a dinner party quickly, as though embarrassed by the act of farewell itself. Yet no one who ever saw him with his grandchildren, or enjoying a Winthrop House musical, or who knew of the quiet pride he took in his students who were teaching English history in most of the major universities in this country, could call him unemotional.

Informality was David Owen's keynote. He dealt with people unaffectedly and directly. Yet he had a profound respect for correct form and proper procedure, as long as he felt that they stood for something truly valuable; just as he was not afraid of emotion, as long as he felt that it was genuine. Thus he would have understood our attempt to do justice to his life and services, just as he would have been pleased by the *Crimson*'s editorial tribute to him on the day after his death: "This gentle professor, who left his Widener office open for thirty years, has served as an example of intellectual generosity that Harvard will not soon forget."

Paul H. Buck   Elliott Perkins
Franklin L. Ford   John Clive, *Chairman*

Memorial Minute
Faculty of Arts and Sciences
December 3, 1968

PROVOST

"An abiding loyalty to Harvard"

PAUL HERMAN BUCK

August 25, 1899 - December 23, 1978

Paul Herman Buck entered University Hall at a trying moment in Harvard's history. In the 1930s, all American institutions of higher education felt the effects of prolonged depression; and the economy in 1939 showed but feeble signs of recovery. Harvard's finances while not as deeply wounded as those of other universities were hardly robust. The student body was internally fragmented; and the faculty seethed with resentment that reflected the continuing vulnerability of its junior members. President James Bryant Conant had made a shaky start and his administration was still in transition. It had just absorbed the implications of the report on tenure by the Committee of Eight, with its thinly veiled criticism of presidential power. Soon the war intervened and removed Conant for long periods of national service in Washington. After Pearl Harbor a large part of the student population took leave for national service and the University found itself engaged in the unfamiliar business of housing and training various branches of the armed forces. At the same time part of the faculty dispersed for assignments

75

connected with the war. To meet these novel challenges, the University relied upon a creaky apparatus of administration, ill-adapted to change.

In 1938, Paul Buck was still an assistant professor. Only in that year did he secure tenure. Yet he had already planted roots in the community and had shaped the abiding loyalty to Harvard which remained with him through the rest of his life. That loyalty and the qualities of his personality served him and the University well in the years that followed.

Paul Herman Buck was born in Columbus, Ohio, on August 25, 1899, around the corner from the public library. He died in Cambridge on December 23, 1978, at the age of 79. He passed his youth near his birthplace, graduated from the Columbus East High School in 1917, then attended the Ohio State University where he earned bachelor's and master's degrees. He may have had moments of uncertainty about his future and about the means of financing his higher education. At the end of his junior year, on June 10, 1920, he secured from the Lake Carriers Association a certificate as ordinary seaman. He never mentioned these credentials in later life; and there is no evidence that he actually served. But he kept the certificate—a memento of his past.

Instead, he embarked upon the study of history. At Harvard where he came to work toward the doctorate, he studied with Arthur Meier Schlesinger, but also with W.S. Ferguson to whose training in Greek history he often referred. An unusually perceptive essay for the master's degree found publication in the *American Historical Review*. More than half a century later, it remained a brilliant source of insight on the southern poor whites. Buck acquired a broad background not only in American but in European history. He spent the year 1925-26 in France and England on a Sheldon fellowship. In Paris he had lived on the Rue Jacob near the Bibliothèque Nationale, in London on Torrington Square near the British Museum, immersing himself in those great libraries. His dissertation, a study of the aftermath of

Reconstruction (1935) published as *Road to Reunion 1865-1900*, and awarded the Pulitzer Prize in history in 1938, was cultural and social history at its best.

Meanwhile, he had been drawn into the service of the University he loved. He learned through experience something of the problems of untenured faculty. Having taught in the Department of History as instructor (1926-1936), assistant professor (1936-1938) and associate professor (1938-1942) he became first, assistant dean and then dean of the Faculty of Arts and Science (1942-1953), in charge of the central instructional and research departments of the University. Buck became provost of the University (1945-1953), then Francis Lee Higginson Professor of History in 1955, and finally Carl H. Pforzheimer University Professor. During the war years he was chief administrative officer of the University while President Conant was away on national service. Later President Conant noted that they had worked as a team for more than a decade. "I happen to have worn the ranking hat, but he carried the load. The initiative, imagination, accomplishment were his."

Buck's first assignment was to clarify the ambiguous relationship to Radcliffe College, introducing the then radical program of joint instruction in the two institutions. Years later, in a paper for the Massachusetts Historical Society, he exposed the ignorance, prejudice and confusion that had from the start clouded Radcliffe's charter which provided for a separate but dependent female institution, one governed by its own trustees except that Harvard voted all degrees and provided all instruction. In practice by the 1920s that meant that professors who wished to do so could earn additional sums by crossing the Square to repeat their lectures to the young ladies, who lived in their own quarters, and used their own library and laboratories. President Lowell, impatient with the whole arrangement, wanted to sever the ties entirely but, yielding to inertia, did nothing. President Conant was more sympathetic and in September 1942 asked the new dean to work out a solution "once and for all"—but one that was financially acceptable.

The process of arriving at a decision revealed the conditions under which the two men worked. Buck had already discussed the issue with Ada Louise Comstock, president of Radcliffe; but Conant spent most of his time in Washington. The dean arranged to get on the train in New York that bore Conant from Washington on December 22, 1942. The uninterrupted four-hour ride to Back Bay enabled them to hammer out the details. Between February and April 1943 Buck secured the approval of the faculty, of the governing boards and of the Radcliffe trustees; and the radical new form of joint instruction went into effect the next academic year. In this as in the other changes in which he led the University, he showed the ability to cut through to the heart of each problem, the imagination to contrive a novel solution and the personal sensivitity that enabled him to extort the acquiescence of others. In 1946 Buck was the moving spirit in the preparation of the report on *General Education in a Free Society* adopted in 1950 as the central element of the undergraduate curriculum. As provost he helped establish the Computation Laboratory, the Russian Research Center, the Department and Laboratory of Social Relations, and the Division of Engineering Sciences (now the Division of Applied Sciences). He became involved too in devising an accommodation in the Arnold Arboretum's tangled affairs. Each was a monumental task in modernizing the structure of an ancient educational system. Through all these changes, however, he and President Conant united in agreement on the central importance of maintaining the excellence of the faculty, a task to which Buck again and again turned his attention.

In the trying years after 1950 when many universities, including Harvard, were under attack from roving congressional committees, clumsily on the search for communists, Buck vigorously defended academic freedom. He insisted on a punctilious case-by-case examination of charges, distinguishing between disloyalty and dissent. His files contain instance after instance in which he fended off unsubstantiated charges. In the one case in which the Corporation considered the dismissal of a tenured member of the faculty, Buck interceded so that the action became a reprimand.

When President Conant resigned in 1953, Buck returned to teaching in the Department of History and to scholarship. He had rejected invitations to the presidencies of a number of other universities, for loyalty to Harvard held him in Cambridge; and he intended to compose a history of the transformation of Harvard College into a university, a project that he believed would enable him to trace the most important strands in modern education. But he had never been a facile writer and the work went slowly, for he held punctilious standards of research. In 1955 therefore he welcomed the opportunity to become director of the Harvard University Library, a position he held until 1964. As dean in 1948-49 he had taken the first steps in reorganizing the structure of an immensely complex, decentralized institution by establishing a budgetary link between the Harvard College Library and the Faculty of Arts and Sciences. As director he reorganized the staff of the world's largest university library, finding the financial means to preserve it as an effective teaching and research tool. In his nine years in office the libraries increased by 1,400,000 volumes while some 14 construction projects provided much needed space. His reflections on those problems appeared in *Libraries and Universities* (1964). He left the library in 1964 in part at least because of disagreement with President Pusey over the character of the Kennedy Library then planned for Harvard. The assassination had shocked Buck as it had others to the point at which he could not consider these problems without emotion.

Outside Harvard, Buck was one of the founders and long a director of the Center for Advanced Study in the Behavioral Sciences. As chairman of the Ford Foundation's Committee on the Role of Education in American

History, he helped stimulate work in a subject he considered important and long neglected. He had also been a member of the Commission on Financing Higher Education and a member of the United States Commission on the Humanities and chairman of its committee on library needs.

Through his other efforts, he retained a lively interest in history, although administrative burdens prevented him from applying his energies to his own work in that field. In addition he suffered silently from recurrent illness. Back in 1938 he discovered his vulnerability to Paget's disease that made any bone fracture difficult to heal; and 20 years later he endured long and painful surgical procedures, after which he was never quite the same again. Nevertheless, his course on southern history continued to attract undergraduates and his seminars on historiography and educational history trained a generation of graduate students. Some of the products of those seminars appeared in the volume he edited, *The Social Sciences at Harvard* (1965). Among his awards were the Pulitzer Prize in history, decorations from France and Greece and honorary degrees from Ohio State, Brown, Tufts, Harvard, Princeton, Coe, and Western Reserve.

Bernard Bailyn   John H. Van Vleck
Douglas W. Bryant   Oscar Handlin, *Chairman*

Memorial Minute
Faculty of Arts and Sciences
March 11, 1979

MASTER OF LOWELL

"High table and sympathy"
ELLIOTT PERKINS
March 16, 1901 - March 4, 1985

Elliott Perkins was born in Westwood, Massachusetts, the son of Thomas Nelson and Louisa Adams Perkins. He graduated from Milton Academy in 1918, after which he spent a year on a Wyoming ranch. Life was rough there; so rough, indeed, that the owners—who had obliged a friend in Boston by letting his son come out for a short period—did not expect to find him still there after they returned from their annual winter sojourn in a warmer climate. But there he was, still roughing it with the cowhands in the bunk house. Rounding up cattle and doing farm chores in arctic temperatures took him a long way from the gentilities of Boston.

The grandnephew of Henry Adams and the son of a member of the Harvard Corporation learned that cowhands were capable of being as amusing and as excellent company as Brahmins, a lesson not without significance in the education of Elliott Perkins. In his characteristically pungent manner, which itself doubtless owed something to his year in the West, he was heard to remark more than once, in later life, that when you haven't had a change of underwear during the winter months, you feel very different.

Perkins entered Harvard College in 1919, just a few months after the faculty, acting on President Lowell's plan for curricular reform, voted to apply across the board degree requirements involving concentration, general examinations, and tutorial. With that vote, Perkins would later recall, "the salvation of Harvard College got fully under way." The old system had meant that "a natural minority threaded its way to excellence, and a bemused majority loafed its way to 'a gentleman's C.'" Under that system, Perkins felt sure, he himself would not have taken honors. Now, challenged by the required generals and thesis in history and literature, and goaded on by his tutor, he graduated *cum laude*.

After two uncongenial years at the Harvard Law School, he "acted on instinct and left the place while I could do so with dignity." His immediate destination was the office of the then dean of the College, Chester Noyes Greenough, a man who believed, as Perkins himself came to believe, that a dean's chief function was to make exceptions to the rules. He would remember his decanal stint as "the delightful pastime of telling others how to avoid the pits into which I had fallen, and watching them fall straight into them."

In 1927 he left the dean's office in order to begin graduate work in history and to start a tutorial connection with history and literature which was to endure for the rest of his academic career. His chief mentors in the history department were Abbott, Haskins, McIlwain, and Morison—all eminent scholars, all fired up about teaching undergraduates, and all, so Perkins would later describe them, amateurs: "That is, they were doing what they were doing because they liked to do it, not because academic achievement brought them financial or social advancement." He approved of that.

Perkins received his PH.D. in 1936. His dissertation, "The Electoral Structure of England in the Time of Sir Robert Walpole," was based on three years of archival work in England, done in large part under the guidance of the great Lewis Namier. He became a faculty instructor in history in 1937, the same year in which he married an Englishwoman from a distinguished family background, Mary Baker Wilbraham, a marriage that proved to be an extraordinarily happy one. He could now put into practice full time one of the guiding ideals of his life, that teaching was the most important thing one could do because teaching was what Harvard was all about.

In 1940 came the incident he never tired of recounting: "A request to wait upon the president one April Tuesday was accepted as an invitation to the customary farewell interview. Nerved to keep a stiff upper lip while concluding 15 years as a Harvard officer, I was completely nonplussed when Mr. Conant offered me the mastership of Lowell House."

Perkins had served his apprenticeship as a House tutor in Lowell House, under Julian Coolidge. Now he was able to impose his own stamp on a House which, for 22 years, was to flourish under his mastership. During that period he became a legend, and legends are hard to disentangle. What was it that made him so successful in his position? That curious mixture of *gravitas* and humor that characterized those elegant notices on the House bulletin board? The way he nurtured his senior common room with paternal pride and solicitude, while consulting it only after the fact? (The essence of a good housemaster, he was heard to remark, was "tyranny untempered, I hope, by assassination.") The respect for custom and tradition that made Lowell House high table, where tutors, students and guests dined together in ever decreasing formal splendor each Monday night, a keystone of House life? Thursday teas, where the tartness of the cucumber sandwiches blended nicely with the grace and warmth of the master and his wife? The master's own persona, as observed by a *Crimson* reporter: "When he walks in the Lowell House courtyard, he has the air of a country squire inspecting his properties"? That limitless supply of human sympathy under what initially struck some House

83

members as a solemn and stern exterior, which led him to spend countless hours counseling and encouraging those students who had personal or academic difficulties?

The obvious answer to those questions is, of course: a combination of all these things. But there is a less obvious answer, no less true. It is to be found in Perkins' class reports in which he dubs the House system Mr. Lowell's culminating reform, and singles out as one of its most important functions that of breaking up the old private school monopoly of College leadership. The Houses, so he writes in his twenty-fifth class report, "have developed a vigorous, independent, and delightful social life of their own." And adds: "Meanwhile, thank God, the Harvard tradition of individuality holds its triumphant sway."

Here is the essence of Perkins' thought and belief: to preserve the best of the old Harvard, while accommodating inevitable changes. Tea and cucumber sandwiches, high table, weekends for all House tutors in turn at the Perkins' beloved North Shore summer retreat at Little River, the Augustan bulletin board, all served that purpose—as well as being enjoyable in their own right. If Harvard College was to continue to be a great institution—and Perkins' faith in the College bordered on the fanatical—then it had to accomplish two things at once: change some of its old ways, while holding on to some of the others.

Though he would have been the last to have been pompous about the matter, Perkins was a man with a mission. On its positive side, that mission emphasized conscientious teaching, human sympathy, respect for eccentricity and wit as well as for good manners and tradition; on the negative side, dislike of snobs and people on the make, of conformism, of newfangled gimmicks. Because he himself had been someone who had, to use one of his favorite expressions, "caught fire" in tutorial, he was always most concerned about those students who, on the basis of early grades alone, might all too readily have been relegated to some nonhonors limbo, but who needed, above all, careful guidance and attention to bring out their latent capacities. As a tutor he would at times surprise a tutee by a remark like: "So you've been reading Gibbon. I haven't read him for years. Tell me about him." The student's initial pleasure at being spared questioning in detail would soon give way to the therapeutic discomfiture of having to attack the root of the matter. Which was, of course, just what Perkins intended.

His lectures on eighteenth-century British history centered on old-fashioned themes: politics and battles. But while his admiration for Walpole was considerable, he did not by any means confine himself to the great and famous. He knew from his own research about politics on the local level, about the workings of patronage, about the emollient effects of free beer and golden sovereigns. And no one who heard his lectures on the British army and navy will easily forget what it meant to advance in line into the deadly fire of the enemy, or to be flogged round the fleet.

His friends called him Perk. What he valued in them was wit, amiability, frankness, and perhaps above all loyalty. And he stood by them through thick and thin. Those who had the good fortune to be among them came to love this proper Bostonian who was very far from conforming to the supposed model of his type; to whom they could talk freely about everything, and on whose sensitivity, understanding, wisdom, and discretion they could invariably count. They will miss him greatly, though memories of the wry grin and the upright carriage with which to the last he strode about the College make his absence a bit easier to bear.

Franklin L. Ford   Maurice M. Pechet
John V. Kelleher   John L. Clive, *Chairman*

Memorial Minute
Faculty of Arts and Sciences
November 12, 1985

85

AMERICANIST

"Intellectual energy prodigious and perpetual"

HOWARD MUMFORD JONES

April 16, 1892 - May 11, 1980

Howard Mumford Jones, historian of American culture, man of letters, and one of the most distinguished humanists of our time, died in Cambridge at the age of 88. Early in his long career he established himself as a major literary and social historian with a fresh and vital approach to his field of inquiry. His *America and French Culture* (1927) placed a new emphasis on the Continental European sources of our national heritage at a time when most Americanists were too exclusively preoccupied with the New England component and its Puritan derivations. Over the next 20 years he wrote a number of substantial essays and monographs on many writers and intellectual movements from the colonial period through the early twentieth century and on the general theory of American literature. His principal American studies, however, appeared much later. Well after his retirement, which he grudgingly accepted at 70, he published his magisterial trilogy: *O Strange New World* (1964), *The Age of Energy* (1971), and *Revolution and Romanticism* (1974). Though the title of the second of these describes the five expansive decades fol-

lowing the Civil War, it appropriately characterized the
man himself, for Howard Jones's intellectual energy was
prodigious and perpetual. At the time of his death,
having completed his *Autobiography*, his eleventh book
since retirement, he was at work on yet another spacious
cultural history, *The Old West: an Unconventional View*, one
of the most vigorous chapters of which presents the
American cowboy, a figure he could appraise with particular zest and sympathy.

Howard Jones was the least parochial of American
scholars, prepared, as he always was, to place his subject,
whether it was a single American author or the whole
United States, in the broadest, most cosmopolitan perspective. And his expertise ranged far beyond our national
boundaries or the narrowed concentration of any single
discipline. He had an impressive command of British
intellectual history and a contagious enthusiasm for the
Victorian novel. He wrote a good deal of original verse,
both lyrical and satiric, and clever parodies of his favorite
poets. As a young man he skillfully translated Heine's
Nordsee and a group of medieval songs, and later he made
a memorable version of the solemn *Dies Irae* of Thomas
of Celano. He prepared bibliographies and study guides,
edited a volume of eighteenth-century plays, and with
his wife, Bessie Zaban Jones, assembled a spirited
anthology, *The Many Voices of Boston* (1975). His *Treasury
of Scientific Prose* (1965), compiled with I. Bernard Cohen,
suggests his keen interest in "natural philosophy" and his
high regard for the masters of technical exposition. And
the book he liked best among his own, *The Harp that
Once* (1937), a biography of Thomas Moore, reflects his
wide knowledge not only of Anglo-Irish literature but
also of the larger European romantic movement. Perhaps
most insistently of all, his many shorter works, collections of essays and public lectures, testify to his tremendous vigor and eloquence as defender of the humanities,
an intellectual drive that persisted to the last. It was the
comprehensive vision of the humanist, perpetually alert
to the interdependency of our world, that prompted a

letter less than two weeks before his death to the editor of the *Journal of the History of Ideas*, declaring the need for a deeper understanding of Chinese ideology and of the ethical assumptions of modern India.

Like Hamlin Garland, whom he served in high-school days as a secretary-typist, Howard Jones was proudly a "son of the middle border." Born in Saginaw, Michigan, on April 16, 1892, he spent his youth in La Crosse, Wisconsin, where he attended normal school before going for his B.A. at the University in Madison. He received his M.A. from Chicago in 1915, but then stubbornly refused to take courses, required for the Chicago doctorate, which he himself had already taught at that institution. Fifteen honorary degrees in later years indicate that the lack of a PH.D. proved no considerable handicap in a teaching career that carried him from Texas to Montana to North Carolina and in 1930 to the University of Michigan.

In 1936, precisely the middle year of his long life, he came to Harvard as one of the principal Tercentenary speakers and here remained as professor of English. Though he quickly acquired a remarkable understanding of New England modes and manners, his roots were distinctly Western, or at least Middle Western, in the world beyond the Alleghenies. If Harvard at the time was largely Eastern, exclusive, and self-contained, Howard Jones helped open it—not without some resistance—to a wider American context. His energy, verve, and mercurial temper, at first disconcerting to some of his more restrained colleagues, endeared him to countless students, who found him both generous and exacting. His intellectual demand on scholarship as on literature was indeed strenuous. Of a writer he mostly admired, he wrote: "Faulkner gave man a soul capable of compassion, sacrifice and endurance, but Faulkner left out intelligence. Future novelists may yet return to accepting intelligence as essential in human nature and add to the democracy of the heart the democarcy of the mind." To all those who worked closely with him Howard Jones's erudition was often intimidating. Yet his kindness of heart was as pervasive as his intellectual rigor. Over the years he contributed much of his own double democracy to Harvard, which, in turn, meant much to him: "If intellectual freedom," he once declared, "has her home anywhere, it is in the Harvard Yard." Within that privileged space, his study, Widener 115, became for many of his students a center and a symbol of the free intelligence. From such a vantage he himself ranged the University collections as few others have done until he had developed the special intimacy with the library, its holdings and organization, that is reflected in his late work as editor of the *Harvard Library Bulletin*.

In 1960 Howard Jones was appointed the first Abbott Lawrence Lowell Professor of the Humanities. The next year, receiving another sort of chair, the armchair presented to staff members after 25 years of service, he remarked with characteristic wit: "Harvard is, so far as I know, the only institution in the country that says to employees of long standing, 'I think you had better sit down.'" But he himself was scarcely willing to sit for long. Though he wrote and published much after his retirement in 1962, he eagerly accepted visiting professorships at the universities of Wisconsin and Jerusalem and at Middlebury College, and he continued his lifelong practice of giving lectures and addresses at assemblies and convocations all across the country, from Maine to California.

Howard Jones attained widespread recognition for his scholarship and public service. He was three times a Guggenheim fellow. He was awarded the Jusserand Medal of the American Historical Association in 1934, the Pulitzer and Emerson prizes in 1964, and the Phi Beta Kappa Medal and Prize in 1973. He served for one year (1943-44) as dean of the Harvard Graduate School of Arts and Sciences, for two years (1959-61) as chairman of the Weil Institute for Studies in Religion and the Humanities, for two terms as a member of the Council of the American Philosophical Society, and from 1944 to

1951 as president of the American Academy of Arts and Sciences. He did much to revitalize the American Council of Learned Societies as its chairman (1955-59), and he worked for a complete reorganization of the Modern Language Association as its president in 1965.

Daniel Aaron	Douglas W. Bryant
Herschel Baker	John P. Dawson

Jerome H. Buckley, *Chairman*

Memorial Minute
Faculty of Arts and Sciences
March 10, 1981

IV. Society

SCHOLAR OF HUMAN RELATIONS

"The social importance of the workplace"

FRITZ JULES ROETHLISBERGER

October 29, 1898 - May 17, 1974

Fritz J. Roethlisberger, Wallace Brett Donham Professor of Human Relations, Emeritus, was associated with the Business School for more than 40 years, and earned an international reputation for distinguished contributions to knowledge about human behavior in organizations.

To most people, the name Roethlisberger is associated with that of the late Elton Mayo in the investigations done a generation ago at Western Electric Company's Hawthorne plant in Chicago. Mayo was then a professor who led the industrial research group; Fritz Roethlisberger was first an assistant, later a collaborator. He became a participant in the Hawthorne project in 1927, and soon afterward joined the HBS faculty as a young instructor, never to leave.

The series of experiments at Western Electric began in 1924 and had been under way for more than three years when Roethlisberger took up his role in them. They stand out today as an important benchmark in investigating the human aspects of business management. For the field of human relations and Fritz Roethlisberger the Hawthorne studies were pivotal.

The project had been started as an effort to explore the relationships among such things as shop lighting, worker morale, and productivity. But satisfactory answers remained elusive. As part of the effort to probe deeper, Roethlisberger joined the research team; under the penetrating questions and perceptive insights which since have become his hallmarks among students, the boundaries of the inquiry were steadily widened.

In this way, the study evolved into a major investigation of worker motivation spanning a total of 11 years. At one point, it encompassed many thousands of employees, some two-thirds of the Hawthorne plant's existing workforce.

The meanings and significance of this long investigation—both in substance and in terms of resarch methodology—were described in 1939 in a book by Professor Roethlisberger and William J. Dickson of the Western Electric staff. That book, *Management and the Worker*, was then prophetically acclaimed by Stuart Chase as "the most exciting and important study of factory workers ever made." Symptomatic of its worldwide impact and the durability of the lessons it contained is the fact that the book is still being reprinted—more than 35 years after it first appeared.

It was perhaps the first fully documented study to go beyond and, in effect, to challenge the scientific management concepts of Frederick W. Taylor. He and others early in the twentieth century were preoccupied with the mechanics of production efficiency. They tended to see assembly-line workers as cogs in a machine.

The Roethlisberger-Mayo Hawthorne researches established, as nothing else had, the social importance of the workplace. That published account of the research and its findings enabled management to see that an industrial organization can also be viewed as a social system, that the behavior and productivity of workers are keyed importantly to their personal and social satisfactions as well as to task engineering, and, as a practical matter, that many measurable benefits derive from taking the workers' informal social systems into account in managing the plant.

"Producing an article at a profit and maintaining good employee relations are frequently regarded as antithetical propositions," Roethlisberger and Dickson wrote in their book. "The results of these studies . . . indicated, however, that these two sets of problems are interrelated and interdependent. The kind of social organization which obtains within a concern is intimately related to the effectiveness of the total organization."

Not only was the book a landmark in management studies, it also set a precedent for in-the-shop fact-finding in research into human behavior in organizations.

Carrying forward the work he had started at Hawthorne, Roethlisberger published other books. One, issued by the HBS Division of Research, was *Training for Human Relations.* Another, *Man In Organization*, pulled together a number of his articles which had appeared in professional journals.

In 1959, in recognition of the international impact of his work, Roethlisberger was selected by the Council of Deans to receive Harvard University's top faculty honor—the Ledlie Prize. Established by the late George Ledlie, newspaper executive and associate of Joseph Pulitzer, the honor is given every two years to the individual at Harvard "who has by research or otherwise made the most valuable contribution to science, or in any way, to the benefit of mankind."

That award was in some measure anticipated by the then dean of the Business School, Donald K. David. In 1950, when Roethlisberger was named to the Wallace Brett Donham professorship, Dean David described him as a "man who set a course for the training of responsible leaders in our democracy and who helped us to see the importance of the individual as a human being both in business and in education."

95

For his part, Roethlisberger was not one to cast himself in a heroic mold. A scholar fully conscious of the changing nature of man's environment, as well as the continuity of man's foibles, he presented findings lucidly, yet responded to every dogma with a question—and a twinkle in his eye that established him as tolerant and friendly.

At his memorial service some of his own words were read to recall his view of those who are spectators of life rather than participants in it. "Many of them," he once said, "were trying to be extraordinary before they had learned to be ordinary." During his last illness he commented to a friend: "The nurses want to be doctors. The doctors want to be surgeons. And the surgeons want to be God. But there's nobody left to fluff my pillow."

His work is still challenging business management "to free the vast amount of frozen human energy that exists in our modern organizations." Only a few years ago, he argued that management had lost touch with the rewards and punishments that determine the satisfactions of workers at all levels. "Management," he said, "must assume the new leadership role of freeing the creative impulses of workers in organizational settings."

Fritz Roethlisberger was born in New York City in 1898, the son of a Swiss father and a French mother, who had emigrated to this country. He was graduated from Columbia University in 1921 with a B.A. degree, to which he added a B.S. from Massachusetts Institute of Technology in 1922 and an A.M. from Harvard in 1925.

He was appointed instructor in industrial research at the Harvard Business School in 1927, assistant professor in 1930, associate professor in 1938, and professor of human relations in 1946. Four years later he was named to the professorship honoring Wallace Brett Donham, the school's second dean. Donham had been instrumental in developing a strong faculty group to study the behavior of men and women in organizations because, as a former banker, he sensed that business ran into difficulty more often as a result of weaknesses in communications and motivation than for any other reason.

In addition to his research contributions, Roethlisberger enjoyed a high reputation as one of the school's great classroom instructors. His teaching was enlivened as he brought to the case discussions a profound knowledge in a range of fields—social psychology, anthropology, semantics, psychiatry in business, and general education—even though he had never taken time out to acquire a doctorate. And although he never earned an M.B.A. either, he was in on the start of as many new programs at the school as virtually any member of the faculty.

He and Thomas North Whitehead started the first second-year M.B.A. course in the field of human behavior. He was one of the original faculty in the administrative practices course; and he had a key role in setting up the courses in the behavioral area for the doctoral program. Roethlisberger also collaborated with Whitehead in the start of what later became the Harvard-Radcliffe program in business administration.

During World War II he had a key part not only in developing the engineering and scientific management war training program, but also in working out part of the education philosophy and curriculum design of the advanced management program, which evolved from the war training program. He also taught as one of the original faculty in the Harvard University trade union program from 1942 to 1946.

One of his colleagues says: "He had a childlike curiosity, like Albert Einstein. He turned others on because of the profoundly naive questions he asked. He continued to help me teach a doctoral seminar in field observation and interviewing right up to the time he went into the hospital. I don't know of any other emeritus professor who maintained such close contact with students."

Fom his pioneering research and widespread influence as an imaginative and inspiring teacher, one might suppose that he would have become the founder of a school of thought or pedagogical approach. Actually, he didn't. Consistent with his belief in the need for accuracy in communications, objectivity in observation, and the essential goodwill of people, he stood, until his death, not only as the dean of the human relations view of management, but also as one of the leading explorers of both the old and new approaches to understanding human behavior.

Commenting on that role, he once said that "it is time we stopped building rival dictionaries to define the concepts of human behavior, and learned to make some sentences that really say something." That theme was reinforced in a book, *Counseling in an Organization: A Sequel to the Hawthorne Researches*, of which he was co-author with William J. Dickson. In it he observed: "What is important is that the spirit of inquiry persists."

Unsigned memoir
Harvard Business School Bulletin
September-October 1974
© 1974 President and Fellows of Harvard College

FACULTY LEADER

"Fidelity to the life of the mind"
MERLE FAINSOD
May 2, 1907 - February 11, 1972

Merle Fainsod, Carl H. Pforzheimer University Professor, was
born in McKees Rocks, Pennsylvania, and moved with his
family to St. Louis, attended
public schools there, and took
his undergraduate degree in
1927 at Washington University. His association with
Harvard began as a graduate
student in government in 1929 and continued unbroken
until his death.

He was a pioneer in the systematic study of communism and the Soviet Union in the western world. His
doctoral thesis, published in 1935 as a monograph *International Socialism and the World War* was concerned with
the origins and background of communism. Believing
from the start that the pursuit of the subject required a
command of the Russian language and firsthand
acquaintance with the country, he made a number of
visits to the Soviet Union, the first on a Sheldon traveling
fellowship in 1932-33, the last in 1970. His interest was
not only scholarly and academic; it extended to the people
who lived under the system and their great national cul-

ture. He loved to observe their everyday life, to browse in bookstores and libraries. Always he was a humanist.

For all his later involvement in teaching and research in American government, Fainsod's warm interest in Russia never abated. Following World War II, he was one of the faculty members most directly responsible for the creation and development of the Russian Research Center, of which he was director from 1959 to 1964. He contributed vitally to making the center not only an outstanding institution of learning but also a happy place to work for those associated with it, whether students, professors, or secretaries.

His magisterial volume *How Russia Is Ruled* appeared in 1953, and was accorded the Woodrow Wilson Foundation award. The academic community recognized that a new standard had been set for the study of the subject. The book was much more than a superb textbook; it was the product of immense erudition, dispassionate yet vigorous in its approach. It manifested the qualities that characterized his course on the Soviet Union: literature, history and economics were summoned to supplement and explain political data. In 1958 his book *Smolensk under Soviet Rule* was awarded the Faculty Prize of the Harvard University Press. It was a brilliant achievement in what might be called political archeology, and is undoubtedly one of the most important works on Russia under communism written since World War II. From the voluminous files of a single Communist Party organization whose archives found their way to the West, Fainsod was able to extract invaluable and hitherto inaccessible data of political and social life in Stalin's Russia. He was able to reconstruct in microcosm Soviet political reality during its formative and previously, for an outsider, largely mysterious period. A projected further major work, on the history of Soviet-American relations, was interrupted by his death.

It may seem odd that this humane and judicious man should become immersed in a field marked by episodes of violence and arbitrariness. And yet it was these qualities of mind, together with a sense of irony and humor, that preserved him from the pitfalls of sensationalism and pedantry. In a field that lay open seductively to pundits and polemicists he remained a scholar of balance and wisdom, who cared deeply about his subject and about his students. For his students he held the gates of learning open wide; he would give them compasses and a chart, and then they took the voyage for themselves, suffering neither benign neglect nor benign paternalism. In every important center of learning in this country there are teachers and scholars in the Soviet field for whom he will remain affectionately not only a model and a mentor, but a figure whose quiet innate moral authority has given an added dimension to their lives.

Given his qualities of mind and character—the catholicity of his sympathies, his measured, selfless judgment, and his capacity for constructive thought—it was natural that he was conscripted for service when conflicting interests called for resolution and reconciliation. His presidency of the American Political Science Association (1966-67) coincided with a period of tensions in that professional group. In 1964 he became director of the Harvard University Library and the first chairman of the University Library Committee. To assess the strengths and the needs of this preeminent collection, subject by subject, to establish sound priorities and attract the necessary resources, was a charge that would tax the range of a scholar and the talents of a diplomat; one had best be a familiar of Aristotle and Maecenas alike. But because the library was at the very center of the University's mission, it was at the very center of Fainsod's concern. The resulting study and report have provided a basis for much library planning in the University, most particularly toward the decision to build the Pusey Library as an essential adjunct to the central library. In this decision and in the appeal for the required funds Fainsod's role was a large one.

His gifts of reconciliation were taxed to the utmost in the aftermath of the crisis in the spring of 1969, when he served as chairman of what came to be known as the Fainsod Committee on faculty reorganization. He spent himself tirelessly and with deep anguish in an effort to resolve cleavages that for a time were unbridgeable. But the report of the committee, however costly it was to him and however far it fell short of his own aspirations, stands as a milestone on the road to reunion.

Fainsod was married in 1933, toward the close of his Sheldon Fellowship, to Elizabeth Stix, of St. Louis. Their circle of friends embraced all parts of the University, and their home in Cambridge was for many a centripetal force that helped to transform a great and diffuse institution into an intimate and caring community. In late years they spent the summer months with their two daughters on Martha's Vineyard. These were seasons of refreshment and quiet study, punctuated on one occasion with explosive anger when a new neighbor was discovered about to cut down a stand of trees near the water's edge. It was an almost unprecedented outburst from the gentlest and most disciplined of men; but there were a few things that could break the bounds of even a saintly toleration.

Merle Fainsod devoted himself without deflection to the advancement of understanding. The responsibilities he undertook for his University and his profession were not digressions from his all-consuming purpose. They were acts of service to the end that conditions might be maintained under which scholarship could flourish more abundantly. His fidelity was always to the life of the mind, for he knew that the duty and the joy of the scholar are, in the end, all one.

Samuel H. Beer   Adam B. Ulam
Douglas W. Bryant   Robert Lee Wolff
          Paul A. Freund, *Chairman*
Memorial Minute
Faculty of Arts and Sciences
May 15, 1972

DEFINER OF THE LEGAL PROCESS

"Philosophical dimensions and historical perspectives"

HENRY MELVIN HART, JR.

December 25, 1904 - March 24, 1979

For almost 40 years I have stood in the circle of enchantment woven by Henry Hart. When I first came to know him, to be sure, I saw him, the august president of the *Harvard Law Review*, through the awestruck eyes of a junior editor. And yet the authority of *Review* presidents is not invariably bewitching, their charisma not inevitably irresistible. It was Henry Hart's formidable intellectual powers, his unswerving commitment to principle, the grace of his pen and the deep-throated charm of his utterance that in rare combination made him a supremely attractive figure and a supremely compelling force.

Two incidents, 40 years apart, will tell the tale. Only a few months ago, when the class in federal courts knew that Professor Hart would take a currently unfashionable position espousing a canon of self-limitation on the part of judges, a group of the ablest students held a caucus and found that they, as men of the hour, were solidly hostile to that position. At the end of the discussion in class the group caucused once more and discovered, to their astonishment, that every one of their number had been converted. They had seen opened up before them philosophical dimensions and historical perspectives that were theretofore outside their range of vision.

I could not help recalling a similar act of conversion in those distant days when Henry Hart was president of the *Review*. Having received from an eminent Philadelphia lawyer an article on shareholders' pre-emptive rights he thought publishable if properly reconstructed, he proceeded to tear it down and build it up, quite transforming it in form and content. When the resulting product was returned for the author's approval, the author responded by sending an explosive letter to Dean Pound demanding that Hart be removed from office forthwith. The dean, of course, disclaimed any jurisdiction over the *Review*, as befitted the relation between two proud and independent sovereigns. There followed a protracted exchange of letters between editor and author, the latter slowly finding himself persuaded to agree on point after point, until finally a letter went again from author to dean, this time urging, if not demanding, that Hart be appointed forthwith to the faculty of the Harvard Law School. That event followed happily after a year spent in postgraduate study with Professor Frankfurter and a year's indelible experience as a law clerk to Justice Brandeis.

In between these episodes of tutelage, the case of the Philadelphia lawyer and that of the classroom skeptics, Justice Frankfurter (as he had become) was himself pleased to go to school to his former well-loved student, though the religious experience of conversion was in this case somewhat harder to achieve. When Henry Hart and his co-author, Professor Herbert Wechsler of Columbia, dedicated their immensely challenging book on *The Federal Courts and the Federal System* to Felix Frankfurter "who first opened our minds to these problems," and sent him a copy of the volume, he penned an acknowledgment that succeeded in stopping a little this side of idolatry.

A copy of the message, dated October 3, 1953, is preserved in the Frankfurter papers:

> When Henry hinted the other night of the problem in truth-telling presented by having the terms of your dedication take due account of my apostasy or at least obtuseness regarding questions of Federal jurisdiction since I came down here, I was prepared to read the following: "Who first opened our minds to these problems, but in his judicial capacity closed his own." Evidently tenderness triumphed over candor . . . [Having spent a number of hours with the book] the overriding feeling that is left in me is one of profound respect for what you have done.

It is no accident, I think, that Henry Hart's interests were centered on procedure. For, as a true disciple of Justice Brandeis, he saw the integrity and fitness of the legal process as a kind of transcendent natural law, a law above laws, standing as the scientific process does to the mutable body of science itself, and reminding us that there is indeed a morality of morality. He taught an early course on legislation at the Law School. He succeeded to Frankfurter's course on the federal courts. He developed the course on the legal process, monumentally conceived, employing telescope and microscope to match the myriad tasks imposed on the legal system against the appropriateness of the various institutions of the system for resolving each of these tasks. In an essay on "The Aims of the Criminal Law," which a distinguished trial judge thought as illuminating as volumes of criminology, Henry Hart insisted that, whatever might be the appropriate form of post-conviction treatment, the criminal process should be brought to bear on conduct if, and only if, the conduct is deserving of moral reprobation. Of this essay, weighty beyond its modest size, and containing some acerbic comments on the insensitivity of the Supreme Court to its truths, Justice Frankfurter wrote, in 1959: "Unlike so many things one reads, it has not only given me pleasure and enlightenment but its stimulus to reflection will not have ceased with the reading of it. I shall duly ponder on the spanking you have given me. . . ."

The impact of Henry Hart on the thousands of students who came under his influence has been enormous. No one could doubt this who has heard his students speak of him as did one of them not long ago when he voiced the utimate tribute: "I feel sorry," he said, "for any student who has not had the course in legal process." No one could witness the anxiety and anguish of his students in his last months as they saw him carrying on against insuperable physical burdens—no one could witness this spontaneous outflow of affection and doubt the persistence of that influence, through oral tradition, through his students who have carried his insights far and wide, and through his writings, which have the enduring quality of a luminous critical framework that long outlives its objects.

Without contrived display, eschewing the shallow arts of showmanship, constitutionally immune to flattery as either a donor or donee, he captivated pupils and colleagues as he had made a spiritual captive of a junior editor 40 years ago.

From a memoir by Paul A. Freund
Carl M. Loeb University Professor
for the service in Memorial Church, March 27, 1969
and later published in the
Harvard Law Review 82:1591 (1969).
© *Harvard Law Review.*

LEADER IN BUSINESS EDUCATION

"Costs, margins and profits"

MALCOLM PERRINE McNAIR

October 6, 1894 - September 9, 1985

Malcolm Perrine McNair, A.B. 1916, A.M. 1920, a native of West Sparta, New York, was a graduate student in the Faculty of Arts and Sciences, working toward a master's degree in English, when he decided to earn some extra money by reading the marketing reports of Business School students for  their English style, correctness and order. McNair's meticulous care and pointed comments so impressed Professor Melvin T. Copeland (who was then in charge of marketing courses and case preparation) that he decided to have young McNair judge the papers for content as well. The next step was an invitation to join the Business School faculty to help with the task of gathering and preparing cases, then in its early stages. Subsequently he became a leading spirit in the effort to develop the case method of teaching business administration, regarding the case as a complex form of literary composition that required the writer to do much more than just present facts to be studied and issues to be resolved.

McNair's own story of his progress, written in 1941, is worth quoting in full:

I have been a pedagogue for more years than I like to remember. Actually the first class I ever faced was a section of Philosophy A at Radcliffe; and I remember taking a long drink of brandy to bolster up my courage before the fateful hour. Subsequently, I was a section hand in Goverment 1 and English A, but my best memories of that time go back to some of the experiences I had assisting "Copey" [the famous English professor, Charles Townsend Copeland] at Harvard and Radcliffe. I am afraid I didn't always get the lamp shade and the windows adjusted precisely right, but it was in those days that I discovered that the real way to learn anything was to try to teach it. As a relief from reading themes and correcting section papers I also dabbled a little in that fascinating enterprise, the Harvard 47 Workshop, and thus came in contact with another great personality of the time, Professor George Pierce Baker [father of the George P. Baker who later became dean of the Business School].

But there wasn't quite enough action to suit me in the conventional academic surroundings; and in 1920, on the spur of the moment, I made a sudden jump from the English Department to the Business School. Then I really came to grips with the kind of teaching and research problems that have fascinated me ever since. I got in on the ground floor of the Business School (in fact, I came in through the back door) and grew up with the institution. My teaching and research work have ranged over the fields of retailing, marketing, and business economics, but in all of these the same challenge has been presented, namely, to help men to learn for themselves by contact with facts and with problems demanding action. The Harvard Business School is probably the least academic educational venture in America. Were it otherwise, I should not be able to find satisfaction in the job.

The work is demanding, but numerous other things also clamor for attention. One or two part-time business connections, occasional consulting work, a little public speaking (mostly in denunciation of current economic heresies), some interesting problems in another phase of university life which I encounter as a syndic of the Harvard Press—all these, on top of the job and the demands of a growing family, leave me shockingly little time for such really important matters as the farm in New Hampshire, trout fishing, deer hunting, very amateur skiing, bad chess, and worse poker.

McNair collaborated in the establishment of the first retailing course at the Business School and taught the subject for some 40 years. During the same period he directed the Harvard Study of Department Store Operating Results, an annual statistical summary of industry progress, financed from the first by the National Retail Dry Goods Association and its successor organization, the National Retail Merchants' Association. McNair's research was chiefly directed at costs, margins and profits, and the development of new methods for the retail sale of merchandise. As a result of this work he was widely known throughout the industry, served as a director of John Wanamaker, Philadelphia, and of Allied Stores Corporation, the national department store chain which includes Jordan Marsh in Boston. He was awarded the Gold Medal of the National Retail Merchants' Association in 1952 and the Converse Award in Marketing in 1953. That year he was also elected to the Hall of Fame in Distribution.

McNair was the school's first director of the Division of Research (1933-36). He wrote or collaborated on *Problems in Retailing* (1937), *Business and Modern Society* (1938), *Problems in Business Economics* (1940), *The American Department Stores, 1920-1960* (1963), and *Controllership in Department Stores* (1965). He was elected the first Lincoln Filene Professor of Retailing in 1950 and retired from teaching as Filene Professor Emeritus on June 30, 1961. In the fiftieth anniversary report of his College class, McNair wrote concerning his philosophy of education:

For most of my life I have considered myself a liberal in educational matters, at least to the extent of advocating and promoting the case method of teaching administration; but I have rebelled against the excesses of the John Dewey "School" and deplore the consequences of the organized educational "racket" in the public schools. In the universities the current emphasis on research and publication, to the extent that it deemphasizes the importance of good teaching, seems to me responsible for some of the unrest among students which recently has made headlines. In my own field of business education I must admit that some of the present-day fashions and fads have passed me by. I think the pendulum has swung too far in the direction both of advanced mathematics and of the behavioral sciences (so-called), at the expense of fundamental training in the exercise of business judgment and initiative.

A powerful and respected figure in Business School affairs under four deans and three presidents, McNair was widely respected for his cogent advice, his stimulating teaching, his frank comments and sound analysis of business conditions. One student profoundly influenced by the bluff and witty professor was James E. Robison, M.B.A. 1940, who as a second-year student was looking for just the right business opportunity. McNair steered him to a friend in the textile business where he thought Robison might find interesting challenges and opportunities. The company, Robison learned, had lost money in 10 of the previous 11 years and it looked, to use Robison's words, "as if there might be some action in the situation." He applied and was hired. Thirteen years later when Robison and his associates decided to set up Indian Head Mills, McNair was invited to join the board of directors. Robison recalled saying to him, "Mac, you got me into the textile business, now help keep me in it." Despite this "outrageous" request, McNair accepted and missed only 3 meetings in 11 years, distinguishing himself as usual by his common sense, his willingness to take risks when there were excellent opportunities for gain, and his characteristic way of asking management "the most embarrassing questions." It was this connection that ultimately resulted in the founding of the Malcolm P.

McNair Professorship of Marketing, given to Harvard as the twenty-fifth reunion gift of the Business School Class of 1940 after a campaign led by Robison.

In 1974, at the age of 80, McNair received the Distinguished Service Award of the Business School, and on October 6, 1984, over a hundred friends and associates gathered at his farm in Madison, New Hampshire to honor "one of the giants of the Business School" (to use Dean Baker's phrase) on his ninetieth birthday. McNair died at Madison eleven months later.

Adapted from a sketch written
by William Bentinck-Smith for the
Directory of Harvard Named Chairs,
in preparation, 1986.

ECONOMIST AND DEAN

"A vein of skepticism about monetary problems"

JOHN HENRY WILLIAMS

June 21, 1887 - December 24, 1980

John Henry Williams was born in Wales and died at the age of 93 in Southbridge, Massachusetts. His long life was a distinguished one embracing careers of teaching and scholarship, mainly at Harvard University, and advice on monetary and financial policy, mainly at the Federal Reserve Bank of New  York, but including services to the departments of State and the Treasury and to numerous international agencies.

He was one of six children, the eldest son, born to John and Margaret Hamer Williams, both of whom came from a long line of farmers in North Wales. Hard times led the family to move south and later to emigrate to the United States, where they settled in a Welsh community in North Adams, Massachusetts. Williams became an American citizen through his father's naturalization in 1900. His academic promise and the personality traits that characterized his later life were evidenced early. He graduated from Drury High School in North Adams at the head of his class in 1904 and had already exhibited outstanding ability as a speaker. In his personal life he was shy and reclusive, with his principal interests in music and roaming the New England woods. When the events of a later highly active life pressed in on him, he found relief from tension in playing the piano and gardening, both lonely activities that removed and protected him from the crowded activities of academic and business life.

Williams attended Williams College for a year and then, like so many later college students, broke off his studies to see a bit of the world. He visited San Francisco after the earthquake of 1906 and then taught for two years in Puerto Rico. On his return, he entered Brown University in 1909 and graduated as valedictorian of his class in 1912. Williams spent the next three years teaching English at Brown.

It can be seen that Williams came late to his chosen field of economics. He entered the Harvard Graduate School in 1915 and, after completing his course work, received a Frederick Sheldon traveling fellowship, which permitted him to spend the academic year 1917-18 in Argentina. From his studies there emerged his doctoral dissertation, "Argentine International Trade Under Inconvertible Paper Money," which received the Wells Prize given for the best economic doctoral dissertation of the year. This study remains a classic in its field. It also led to his appointment as assistant chief, Latin American Division, U.S. Department of Commerce in 1918, where he pioneered what became annual studies of the balance of payments of the United States. His life in government was, however, short. He became an instructor in economics at Harvard in 1918-19; was an assistant professor of economics at Princeton, 1919-20; an associate professor of banking, Northwestern University, 1921 to 1925; and returned to Harvard as an associate professor of economics in 1925. He became a full professor in 1929 and held the position of Nathaniel Ropes Professor of Political Economy from 1933 to 1947, when he became the first Dean of the Graduate School of Public Administration at Harvard.

Williams was a superb teacher of both undergraduates and graduate students. As a young instructor at the time, he gave by far the most polished lectures in his large undergraduate course in money and banking of anyone in the department. As a speaker to large groups, Williams was, indeed, something of a phenomenon. He always spoke without notes, articulating in rounded sentences a carefully structured argument, however complex the subject matter. As his secretary at the Federal Reserve Bank of New York observed, after delivering a speech to a large audience, Williams would return to the office and dictate a manuscript that, with very few corrections, was ready for publication.

As a teacher of graduate students, he followed a quite different procedure. Here he raised questions and was highly successful in inducing the participation of his students in discussions in which it was never quite clear what the position of their interlocutor was. Indeed, it was in these discussions that Williams' positions took forms frequently to appear later in his writings. As one of his students (a governor of the Federal Reserve System) observed, "In class, and even more in conversation, one could see his ideas taking more precise form as he talked. It was the creative process at work in a man with a modest and friendly manner, never very positive yet personally always somehow assured."

Williams' academic activities centered at Harvard, but his principal outside connection was with the Federal Reserve Bank of New York. He was an economic adviser to the bank from 1933 to 1956, vice president in charge of research from 1936 to 1947, and economic consultant, 1956 to 1964. Although he was brought into the bank by President Harrison, his closest connection was with President Alan Sproul, for whom he was an intimate adviser. Williams' usual practice was to spend two days a week in New York attending the officers' council on Wednesdays and directors' meetings on Thursdays, speaking freely in both meetings.

The amount of time he spent in New York got him into some difficulties with the University administration, but on the whole, it proved a fruitful connection, invigorating both his teaching and research. As director of research at the bank, he brought into the bank some of his ablest graduate students, and he brought back to his teaching a lively appreciation of the central problems in monetary and foreign-exchange policy. There is no doubt that Williams enjoyed very much his New York connection. He took advantage of his visits to become active in the affairs of the Council on Foreign Relations. He became a director for the period 1955 to 1964 and was a frequent participant in a number of the council's study groups.

If Harvard found something to cavil at in his New York connections, the bank on occasion objected to the independence of his position on various monetary and foreign exchange policies. This was particularly true on the occasion of the national debate on the Bretton Woods arrangements, particularly the proposed International Monetary Fund. Williams was intensely interested in these proposals and had his research staff at the bank and his graduate students at Harvard working extensively on the issues involved. In fact, he became the leading critic of the proposed fund, publishing his views in a series of articles in *Foreign Affairs*.

Williams espoused what became known as the "key currency" approach, in contrast to the IMF proposal to bring all currencies of the member countries under the scrutiny and influence of the fund. He was much impressed by the fact that most of the international trade of the world was financed in dollars and pounds sterling and considered what happened to the stability and flexibility of these currencies to be critical to the future of the world trade and international capital movements. Indeed, there was much to be said for his position.

In the 1930s a gift to Harvard from Lucius Littauer made possible the establishment of the Graduate School of Public Administration, and Williams was chosen as its first dean. It was the opinion of President Conant and his advisers that the new school should not have a faculty of its own but should draw from various departments of the

University, and that its student body, initially at least, should be drawn from existing government officials. This pretty much assured that the school would remain small and that it would be dominated by the principal contributing departments, in this case economics and government.

Williams was dean of the school for 10 years, and these years were interrupted by the Second World War. The school barely got off the ground during his administration, and there is not much evidence that he was in fact seriously interested in preparing people for the public service. He was primarily a policy-oriented economist, and the principal jewel of the school during his years was a seminar in monetary and fiscal policy which he gave with Professor Alvin Hansen.

This seminar was, during the period immediately after the war, the principal center in the country for the discussion of questions of monetary and fiscal policy. Williams and Hansen were perfect foils for this task and between them trained a fair share of those who are now the leading practitioners in the field. Hansen was an enthusiastic Keynesian, sure of the capabilities of fiscal policy to maintain the aggregate demand needed for full employment. Williams was more of what would now be called a monetarist and was much more skeptical than Hansen of the policies needed to maintain full employment and price stability.

His skepticism of current and received theories and his tendency to "look all around a problem" are expressed in his presidential address to the American Economic Association in 1951:

> A fair question is how much does one's thinking lead and direct, and how much does it merely follow changes in the environment. Very much of the literature of economics strikes me as rationalization after the fact.
>
> I cannot remember when policy questions did not present themselves to me as dilemmas, which I would have to go outside formal theory to get my bearings on, and even then would find very heavy going.

My difficulties may be due in part to an innate attitude of mind which seems always to have included a vein of skepticism and a desire to look all around a problem, rather than plunge forthwith to a bold solution.

Although Harvard and the New York Federal Reserve Bank were the major centers of Williams' activity, he was frequently called on for assistance and advice from other quarters. He was one of two U.S. delegates on the agenda committee for the World Economic and Monetary Conference in Geneva and London, 1932 and 1933. He was head of the State Department mission to investigate Latin American exchange problems in 1934. Williams was an occasional consultant to the Organization of European Economic Cooperation in Paris from 1948 to 1950 and a consultant to the U.S. Economic Cooperation Administration (ECA) in Paris and London, May to July 1949. He was a member of the ECA Advisory Committee on Fiscal and Monetary Problems, 1948 to 1951, and a member of the U.S. Committee on Foreign Economic Policy (the Randall Commission), 1953 to 1954.

His body of writing was not large but included, in addition to his doctoral dissertation, such important works as *Post-War Monetary Plans and Other Essays* (1944), *Economic Stability in the Modern World* (the Stamp Memorial Lecture, London, 1952), *Trade, Not Aid: A Program for World Stability* (1953), and a collection of essays *Economic Stability in a Changing World* (1953). Williams' very real influence in the field of money and banking and financial policy was principally exerted through his advice to actors on the scene and through the large numbers of his distinguished students. There is no doubt that this influence made him a central figure in the fields of domestic and international finance from 1930 to 1970.

James S. Duesenberry   John V. Lintner
             Edward S. Mason, *Chairman*

Memorial Minute
Faculty of Arts and Sciences
November 9, 1982

PHYSICIAN TO CHILDREN

"A teaching life for the sake of the young"
CHARLES ALDERSON JANEWAY
May 26, 1909 - May 28, 1981

Charles Alderson Janeway came from a distinguished medical family; both his father and grandfather were academic clinicians. The grandfather, Edward G. Janeway, was a distinguished consultant in New York City, as well as a part-time professor of pathology and dean of the Bellevue Medical School,  precursor to the New York University Medical School. He is perhaps best remembered today for his description of the Janeway spots, diagnostic of bacterial endocarditis. Janeway's father, Theodore C. Janeway, was an equally prominent internist and became the first full-time professor of medicine at the Johns Hopkins Hospital.

Charles Janeway graduated from Milton Academy in 1926 and received an A.B. degree from Yale four years later. The first two years of his medical education were spent at Cornell; he then transferred for his two clinical years to Hopkins. After obtaining an M.D. degree there in 1934, he came to the Fourth (Harvard) Medical Service of the Boston City Hospital for two years in internal medicine and then returned, for his final year of medical residency, to his alma mater in Baltimore. His formal clinical training having been completed, he and his family came back to Boston in 1937 to embark on two years of scientific training in bacteriology in Professor Hans Zinsser's department at Harvard Medical School. Here his great enthusiasm and interests in the question of respiratory bacteria and his sensible ideas about immunity struck all who worked with him.

It was felt that he had much capacity for these subjects and would do well with them subsequently in the laboratory and clinic. In 1939, he became a member of the staff at Peter Bent Brigham Hospital and was responsible there for the infectious disease service and research under the new Hersey Professor, Dr. Soma Weiss, an old friend from Boston City Hospital days.

Two very untimely deaths occurred at the Harvard Medical School in the early 1940s that were, in good part, responsible for a radical change in Charles A. Janeway's career, catapulting him, to use his own words, from medicine into pediatrics. First, Kenneth Blackfan, Thomas Morgan Rotch Professor of Pediatrics and physician-in-chief at the Children's Hospital, died in 1941; then in January of 1942, Soma Weiss, physician-in-chief at the Peter Bent Brigham Hospital, passed away.

The wise men at the Medical School and the Children's Hospital started grooming Janeway to take over Dr. Blackfan's position by appointing him in 1942 assistant professor of pediatrics; and then, after four years of on-the-job training he became the Thomas Morgan Rotch Professor of Pediatrics and physician-in-chief at the Children's Hospital. He filled this post with distinction for 29 years, bringing honor to his medical school, his hospital, and himself. He retired as physician-in-chief of the Children's Hospital Medical Center in 1974.

For almost three decades Janeway ran the largest academic pediatric service in the United States. Under his aegis, the hospital developed from an active general hospital for children into what we today call a tertiary care center, with 19 divisions in the Department of Medicine alone. It is important to stress, as one of his disciples put it, that human health and illness for Dr. Janeway was a "seamless whole" from biology to behavior. For him, there were no disciplinary boundaries in science.

As an expression of this philosophy, one should mention that among the divisions established by Dr. Janeway were not only the somatic ones like hematology, nephrology, cardiology, etc., but also child psychiatry, an adolescent unit, and a family health care program. The concept of the Children's Hospital Medical Center, with its multidisciplinary programs housed in imposing new buildings, represented the results of fruitful collaboration between the medical staff, led by Dr. Janeway and Dr. Sidney Farber, and the trustees, under J. Wells Farley, taking advantage of the federal government's burgeoning support for the health of children.

Janeway began his career in biochemical science as the United States was approaching its involvement in the Second World War. By 1942 he had published over a half-dozen papers on the uses and mode of action of sulfonamides. With the advent of the war, he joined the large plasma protein fractionation program led by Professor E.J. Cohn.

Janeway was first involved in the use of concentrated solutions of human serum albumin as a plasma expander in shock. Toward the end of the war, he began to explore, and demonstrated, the uses of gamma globulin concentrates in the prevention and attenuation of measles and hepatitis. At the end of the war, when he moved from the Peter Bent Brigham Hospital to the Children's Hospital Medical Center, his interests turned to the plasma proteins in the childhood nephrotic syndrome. He produced foreign protein nephritis in rabbits and showed that irradiation and nitrogen mustards could prevent the disease and that the serum complement was involved in the production of nephritis.

In 1950 he joined Dr. David Gitlin in a series of studies that now stand as classic works on the metabolism of the serum globulins, lipoproteins, and albumin. At about the same time, agammaglobulinemia was discovered by Charles A. Janeway in collaboration with Bruton and Gitlin. The pathogenesis and complications of this first-recognized immunodeficiency disease were reported in the late 1950s. During the next decade, still in collaboration with Gitlin, and subsequently with Fred Rosen, a number of other primary specific immunodeficiency diseases were described for the first time.

The third area of his major influence was in pediatric education. Through his unparalleled leadership, he attracted well over 1,000 superior young people to his house staff and trained them as generalists, subspecialists, and leaders of academia. For the United States and developing countries, he established a model for a training program that included not only scientific discipline, intellectual honesty, and, above all, personal integrity, but also human compassion. He led his students by example to remember always that the sick child and his or her family, rather than the ego-satisfaction or career development of the physician, was the purpose of the effort. He was a humanist first and foremost; indeed, this might well have been the most important thing that he imparted to his pupils.

It has been said that Dr. Janeway truly was the pediatrician of the world. For over two decades, he was a leading figure in international pediatrics, deeply involved with the International Pediatric Association. He was chairman of its executive committee for seven years. He was a wonderful chairman, intelligent, tactful, constructive, and ready to accept sensible compromises as long as the general direction of the activities did not deviate from the prime goal: improved health for all children.

In addition to his activities in the IPA, he was a member of the board of the International Children's Center in Paris, helped establish a new and modern medical school in Shiraz, Iran, and spent two sabbaticals in India. He even had a children's hospital named for him in St. Johns, Newfoundland. His last international effort, which he took on after he retired as chief at Children's Hospital Medical Center, was the development of a new medical college in Cameroun with its community base in small towns and villages.

About Dr. Janeway as a person, one must speak first of Mrs. Janeway, the most important influence on his life and career. They were married 49 years and raised four children who understood and supported his feeling that, in effect, all the children of the world, in their father's mind, were their siblings. Besides this very important part of the man, one recalls at once his objectivity, sometimes frightening, always inspirational. He was always considerate, always trying to see the other side of the question. He was simple, unpretentious, at times even austere. His patience was always exemplary; to be sure, he did get angry, given the circumstances of his job, but he would never show it. He constantly assumed that everybody always acted from the best of motives.

Janeway said in the Thayer Lecture delivered at the Johns Hopkins Hospital in November of 1978, "As physicians and particularly as pediatricians, we have a major responsibility to assure preservation of the integrity of our genetic endowment and an obligation to preserve those natural processes by which life has been sustained on earth by renewable cycles. To overcome this, we must have the courage to include social sciences, genetics, ecology, as sciences of fundamental importance to medicine and health, to think boldly about the organization of government and of our whole commercialized, acquisitive, and consumptive society which provides so well for some of our people, but not for all, with little thought for preservation rather than exploitation of natural resources which cannot be renewed."

William Berenberg	Robert Haggerty
William Castle	David Nathan
John Enders	Fred Rosen

Alexander S. Nadas, *Chairman*

Memorial Minute
Faculty of Medicine
December 15, 1982

FRESH VOICE IN JURISPRUDENCE

"Stimulating speculation about the law"

LON LUVOIS FULLER

June 15, 1902 - April 8, 1978

Lon Luvois Fuller was one of the great law teachers and legal scholars of our time. An active law teacher for 46 years, first at Oregon, Illinois, and Duke, he spent the final 33 years of his active career, from 1939 to 1972, at the Law School.

Fuller was born in Texas and brought up in the Imperial Valley in California. He took his undergraduate and law degrees at Stanford, the latter in 1926, and immediately started teaching. His only period of practice was during the war, when he took the Massachusetts bar examination at the age of 40 and entered active law practice with a Boston firm, much of it in the field of labor arbitration, where he proved himself skillful and effective.

Fuller was a natural teacher, vigorous yet kindly. He set high standards, but terror was never an element of his method. His "bread and butter" course was contracts, to which he must have introduced several thousand of the nation's lawyers. He had written his own case book, which was highly regarded, though it started out with some of the most difficult problems in the field.

Fuller's greatest impact may have been in the field of jurisprudence, which he pursued and illuminated throughout his career. From 1910 to 1940, the teaching of jurisprudence at Harvard was done by Roscoe Pound, who was one of this community's great figures. Through his writings and lectures, Pound did much to transform American legal thinking. There were limitations in his work. Perhaps due to his early work in botany, he carried his taxonomic approach to the law and was a great classifier. This approach was strong in his classroom lectures, given only to graduate, not undergraduate law students.

But Pound was a mighty man, and a great legal thinker. He was a hard act to follow. Fuller did follow him, being appointed to Pound's chair as Carter Professor General Jurisprudence in 1948. He did not seek to emulate Pound. His approach was entirely different. For Fuller succeeded in teaching jurisprudence to substantial numbers of undergraduate law students, and thereby introduced a ferment into the thinking of the general student body which greatly contributed to the teaching of the School. *The Case of the Speluncean Explorers* (1949) is simply one example of this impact.

American law schools have generally not been noted for their teaching of jurisprudence. It was Fuller's achievement that he reached more American law students and stimulated more speculative thought about the law than any other American law teacher. His forte was his interest in undergraduate law students. In *The Law in Quest of Itself* (1940), he wrote:

> The problem addresses itself finally to the law student.
> . . . Shall he search out the professor who can expound
> "the existing law" . . .? Or shall his preference be for
> the man who can impart an insight into the shifting
> ethical background of the law, a background against
> which "the law as it is" appears as an accidental config-
> uration without lasting importance? A similar problem
> of choice confronts him in directing his own studies.
> The way in which the law student decides these questions
> transcends in importance its effects on his own career,

for, through the subtle pressures he exerts on his instructors to teach him what he thinks he ought to be taught, he exercises an influence on legal education—and indirectly on the law—much greater than he has any conception of.

Fuller made many other contributions to legal education. He was a strong member of the faculty with great influence at faculty meetings and other gatherings of law teachers. As chairman of the committee on legal education from 1944 to 1947, he was chiefly responsible for its report which materially affected teaching at the Law School for the next decade or more. He urged a shift away from the consideration of appellate decisions, which were often the end product of failed legal planning, to a more thorough consideration of "client counseling," where the lawyer could uncover the real nature of the client's legal problem and take steps to resolve or avoid it without eventual litigation. Fuller was skeptical of organized legal research and strong in his belief that no one should be under any sort of pressure to undertake it. He was, indeeed, a legal thinker, and felt that only the individual legal scholar, stimulated from within, was likely to do that sort of thinking.

Above all, Lon Fuller was a great human being, firm yet modest, perhaps too modest for his own good. We were inspired by his presence among us, we mourn him, and we give thanks for his many contributions to our thought and life.

A memoir by Erwin N. Griswold,
Langdell Professor of Law (1950-67)
and Dean of the Harvard Law School (1946-69),
published in the *Harvard Law Review*. 92:351 (1978).
© *Harvard Law Review*.

V. The World Around Us

CHEMIST

"Vigorous force in Harvard affairs"
GEORGE BOGDAN KISTIAKOWSKY
November 18, 1900 - December 7, 1982

George B. Kistiakowsky began an adventurous, vibrant, and highly successful career in Kiev, Russia, the son of a professor of international law. At his death on December 7, 1982, he was Abbott and James Lawrence Professor of Chemistry Emeritus at Harvard.
Kistiakowsky was an eminent scientist, a very loyal officer of this University, and a tireless battler for the proper application of science to public policy questions. In particular, he continued his vigorous crusade for the control of nuclear weapons right up to his last days.

His friends knew him as a truly exceptional man, courageous, dashing, witty, intelligent, and strong. Kistiakowsky was fearless and forceful in expressing his views, in public as well as in private. He held strong opinions about people as well as issues so that he inevitably made enemies, but he never let this interfere with his advocacy of courses of action he believed in. In fact, he seemed to thrive on controversy. Each of us has his favorite Kistiakowsky story, all marked by his unique brand of irreverent humor, which never left him.

After a series of hair-raising adventures as a member of the White Army in the Russian Revolution and a harrowing escape from the Crimea, Kistiakowsky's scientific career started in Berlin. There he began his lifetime study of chemical kinetics—the detailed steps by which chemicals react—under Professor Max Bodenstein, from whom he acquired his approach to chemical research: the primacy of experiment and the importance of a personal command of a broad range of laboratory and intellectual techniques.

Brought to Princeton in 1926 by Hugh Taylor, he contributed to the intense activity there in catalysis and photochemistry as branches of kinetics. He also chalked up a "first" by demonstration (with W.T. Richards) that the velocity of sound could be used, as had been predicted by Einstein, to measure the rates of fast reactions.

After J.B. Conant, then chairman of the chemistry department, lured him to Harvard in 1930, he revitalized physical chemistry here and began his long service as a teacher, an internationally known research scientist, and a most effective member of the Department of Chemistry.

His deep interest in physical chemistry was not limited to kinetics and led him to make significant contributions to other areas. An example is the analysis of the rotational fine structure of the ultraviolet spectrum of formaldehyde (a work on which a leading tool for molecular structure determination was built).

Another illustration was the initiation and successful execution of a large program of thermodynamic measurements in part based on heats of hydrogenation instead of the traditional heats of combustion. His new methodology gave the extra accuracy needed to verify a leading and then controversial chemical theory, the theory of resonance. Part of the data from the same program helped show that there are usually forces acting inside molecules that restrict their capability to coil and uncoil freely, a concept crucial for the understanding of proteins.

His group was responsible for the measurement of the rates at which changes (known as cis-trans interconversions) occur in the geometry of certain organic compounds, and led to a quantitative understanding of the thermal stability of such compounds. These examples were also characteristic of his outlook: they all dealt with important unsettled questions and required very definite advances in technique for their success. It should be noted that most of these techniques involved ultimately the hands-on personal attention of Kistiakowsky to rescue an inexperienced student by providing the logical analysis of the difficulties, or the intuitive command of the situation needed to choose the right path. Perhaps sometimes his help could have been used earlier, but when he brought it to bear, everyone around knew that a major action was taking place.

His program of developing measurement techniques for the shock tube (a pipe down which an explosive wave or a steep pressure wave could be propagated) enabled chemical reactions to be studied under bizarre conditions of temperature and speed. Wholly different was the work with his student Herbert Gutowsky (authoritatively aided by George Pake and Edward Purcell), which was the first attempt to apply nuclear magnetic resonance (NMR) to chemistry. Today NMR is absolutely crucial in chemistry and is now beginning to be applied to humans for medical diagnostic purposes.

Although Kistiakowsky is credited with a remarkable number of original studies spread over an unusually broad range of fields, he always returned to his central interest, chemical kinetics. Thus, he and Robert Gomer developed the then novel but now standard method of pulsed photodissociation and so determined the absolute rate of recombination of two methyl radicals, a fundamental result that has proved most useful for determining rates of other free-radical reactions. He also initiated a series of studies of the behavior of methylene radicals, a field of great activity to this day.

He achieved these scientific accomplishments in close collaboration with the many—over 100—superlative graduate students and postdoctoral fellows that Harvard attracts. His highly informal coffee breaks were a joyous forum for discussions of chemistry and a broad range of other topics. His classroom teaching was mainly in chemical thermodynamics and introductory physical chemistry, where he was not averse to the use of pyro-technics to capture his students' attention.

Kistiakowsky's wisdom, judgment, and decisiveness made him a powerful leader in the councils of the chemistry department, especially during his chairmanship. His participation greatly enhanced the standing of the department worldwide. He was also a strong force in University affairs. For example, he led a very controversial campaign to revise the admissions procedures of Harvard College, which he felt were biased against students interested in science; at the same time, he very happily served on the committee on athletics.

In 1941, with Hitler's armies sweeping all before them, Kistiakowsky joined in a program to fill the huge gaps in the U.S. capability for defense. The sinking of ships by submarines in sight of our coasts was finally stopped by new technological developments. One among these was the acceptance by the Navy of a new and more powerful explosive called RDX that was introduced by the British. The American product was manufactured by a new process, was effectively desensitized to avoid accidents, and thoroughly tested in the air and in water by scientists working in programs that Kistiakowsky, as chief of the explosives division of the National Defense Research Committee, helped plan, and for which he was ultimately responsible. Later, he transferred to Los Alamos where his section developed the explosive lens for the atomic bomb. He himself assembled, with his own hands, the device for the awesome first nuclear explosion at Alamogordo.

The memories of that event never left him as his career in and out of government gradually turned him into a full-time crusader for the control of nuclear weapons.

He became the trusted science advisor of President Eisenhower and was thrust, not unwillingly, into the battle then raging over the test ban issue and the initiation of a government agency set up to coordinate the technical, political and military issues of nuclear disarmament. Although arms control and national security matters were dominant concerns, Kistiakowsky took special pride in promoting policies to support science education and basic research. This period is documented in his published diary, *A Scientist at the White House.*

The Vietnam War pushed him more deeply into public policy questions. At first he agreed to advise the military in an effort to deescalate the war and reduce the bombing of North Vietnam. He was actively involved in developing the so-called "electronic fence" intended to keep men and supplies from entering South Vietnam. Eventually he felt that this plan was being sabotaged by the military. This triggered his vocal and full opposition to the war and his complete resignation from all his numerous federal advisory posts.

In 1965 he was elected vice president of the National Academy of Sciences (having refused to allow his name to be put in nomination for the presidency). His two terms in this office were extremely important for the academy. He set up its main group for the study of truly major public issues, such as the world population problem. He also very significantly revised the machinery for reviewing academy reports, making them more responsible and less subject to bias. Evidently, his forthrightness and dedication did not decrease with age.

It is hard to understand how Kistiakowsky managed to combine in one life so much original research, so much teaching and guidance to his graduate students, such fun in skiing and sailing and all aspects of life, yet such a great amount of most effective public policy activity.

In 1977 he accepted the chairmanship of the Council for a Livable World, an organization devoted to the prevention of nuclear war. He threw himself into this activity with characteristic energy and effectiveness. The risk of total destruction of the human race has probably never been greater, but at least there is an increased awareness of the danger, thanks to a handful of people like George Kistiakowsky.

A long list of prestigious medals and prizes, honorary degrees and memberships in learned societies acknowledged his accomplishments. He received, among other awards, the Presidential Medal for Freedom, the Exceptional Service Award of the Air Force, the National Medal of Science, the Parsons Award for Outstanding Public Service, and the Nichols, Willard Gibbs, Richards, and Debye awards of the American Chemical Society for his scientific achievements. He was elected a foreign member of the Royal Society and received honorary degrees from Harvard, Oxford, Princeton, University of Pennsylvania, Carnegie Institute of Technology, Williams, Columbia, Brandeis, and other universities.

J. Kenneth Galbraith   William Klemperer
Dudley Herschbach   Frank H. Westheimer
E. Bright Wilson, *Chairman*

Memorial Minute
Faculty of Arts and Sciences
November 13, 1984

CRUSADER FOR PUBLIC HEALTH

"True citizen of the world community"

HUGH RODMAN LEAVELL

November 7, 1902 - August 7, 1976

Hugh Rodman Leavell was born in Louisville, Kentucky, the son of a physician, Hugh Nelson Leavell. After attending the University of Virginia, from which he received a B.S. degree, he entered Harvard Medical School and graduated with the M.D. degree in 1926. Then followed seriatim internships at  the Massachusetts General Hospital, the Presbyterian Hospital in New York City, and Johns Hopkins Hospital where he remained for an additional year as an assistant resident. Following this, the first phase of his varied and illustrious professional career began.

Simultaneously, in his native Louisville, he set up a private practice, became an instructor at the University of Louisville School of Medicine, and accepted the position of director of public health. So, from the very outset, his interests involved the whole of medicine and its relation with the whole community. This beginning was truly an earnest of his future professional development. In 1938 he became professor and head of the Department of Public Health at the University of Louisville and soon thereafter, in 1940, completed the DR.P.H. degree at Yale

135

under the distinguished guidance of Professor Charles Edward Amory Winslow. Following a brief tour of duty with the United States Public Health Service during World War II, as deputy director of health, European Regional Office of the United Nations Relief and Rehabilitation Administration, and a one-year period as assistant director of the Division of Medical Sciences of the Rockefeller Foundation, the second major phase of his career began at the Harvard School of Public Health.

Early in 1946 the School of Public Health became a separate administrative unit of Harvard University, with a full-time dean and a faculty of its own, independent of the Medical School. Later that year, Leavell was invited to join the faculty as professor and head of the Department of Public Health Practice, a position he retained until his retirement in 1963. During most of his tenure he served also as assistant dean of the school.

Leavell's concept of public health was a very broad one that embraced all relevant disciplines, all levels of practice, and all parts of the world. He believed unswervingly in the potentialities and values of public health practice and worked tenaciously and continually for its acceptance as an academic discipline. This comprehensive view was reflected in his teaching and in the directions he gave to the development of his department. To encompass such an extensive spectrum of activities necessitated not only the involvement of a multidisciplinary team but also an understanding of and identification with community agencies and groups of all kinds. Therefore, the composition of his departmental faculty and staff reflected these broad interests. Early in his headship he had brought medical care teaching into the program with the appointment of the late Franz Goldmann, and soon thereafter he instituted a health education unit. Then, long before it was accepted practice, a social science unit was established in his department to give emphasis to the psychological, social, and cultural factors impinging on health. In quick succession, he developed a community mental health unit and a gerontology unit, both well staffed and well funded.

The community mental health unit recruited a multidisciplinary team drawn from psychiatry, psychology, psychiatric social work, nursing, and the social sciences. This group taught the general public health students the potential mental health implications of their future work so that they might play an effective part in designing, operating, and evaluating community programs for the prevention and control of mental disorders. Perhaps an even more important contribution was fostering innovative developments in the thinking and practice of the mental health staff he had recruited. He collaborated with the late Erich Lindemann in establishing the pioneer multidisciplinary Wellesley Human Relations Service, which became a prototype for the community mental health centers that were organized a decade later throughout the country and are now a widely used model in the western world.

The mental health specialist faculty, most of whom had come to the school from an individual-patient-oriented clinical setting, learned from Dr. Leavell such concepts and skills as acceptance of responsibility to control disorders in a bounded population, populations at risk, levels of prevention, setting priorities, planning services in relation to the ascertained needs of populations, and building coordination among community agencies. What the mental health specialists learned from Leavell was used to develop a body of theory and of practice skills which has become the foundation of community mental health as we know it today. It was included in the 1963 Federal Community Mental Health Centers Act and its subsequent amendments.

Leavell's team concept involved not only specialty groups focused on specific problems, such as mental health and gerontology, but also other specialty groups whose skills and competencies were relevant to the solution of more generic community health problems, like social workers, nurses, health educators, social scientists, local and state health administrators, members of the faculties of the Harvard Business School, the Laboratory of Social Relations, the Graduate School of Education, the Littauer Center, and the Heller School of Social Welfare of Brandeis University. In addition he included faculty members in other departments of the School of Public Health. All these and others were intimately involved in implementing his program concepts and content. His efforts at melding a wide spectrum of apposite expertise were unceasing and circumvented the usual barriers interposed by domain preservation, academic status considerations, and institutional constraints; for his constantly demonstrated belief was in the kind of teamwork that is built "on respect for the essential contributions of other professions and on understandings of their professional strivings," to use his own words.

What an innovative, inspiring, imaginative and stimulating teacher he was! Always ready to try the untested such as: team field teaching studies in partnership with a variety of community agencies; the case study approach; small group methods, with community staff and faculty serving together as resource persons; problem-solving focused on real-life issues and programs; vigorous student participation in all aspects of curriculum development, program planning and implementation. He displayed consummate skill in developing his staff and students, in defining and clarifying the concepts to be taught, in utilizing resource materials and personnel, and in challenging students and staff to think creatively and independently.

Leavell made numerous contributions to local, state, national, and international agencies and programs. He served as president of the Massachusetts Public Health Association, the American Public Health Association, the National Health Council, and the Association of Schools of Public Health—the only non-dean ever to hold this latter office.

While serving as president of the American Public Health Association and of the Association of Schools of

Public Health, Leavell organized a concerted campaign in Washington, on behalf of schools of public health, enlisting endorsements by governors, mayors, civic organizations, and influential citizens, and working closely with key members of the administration and Congress. The result was enactment of the Hill-Rhodes Act of 1958, landmark legislation that provided formula grants and subsequently construction funds that permitted not only program expansion and enrollment increases in the 10 existing schools of public health but also the eventual creation of 11 new schools.

In 1961, the Massachusetts Public Health Association presented to him its Lemuel Shattuck Award for outstanding achievements in promoting public health in New England and cited him for his "administrative talents fundamentally grounded on an unusual group of human relationships." In 1970, he was the recipient of the American Public Health Association's Sedgwick Memorial Medal.

Leavell was a true citizen of the world community. With Dean James Stevens Simmons, he inaugurated the Bridge of Health Mission and in that enterprise traveled around the world during the 1950s visiting the health ministries of other nations in an effort to establish cooperative health programs. During 1956 and 1957, he served actively in India as consultant to the Ford Foundation, establishing village-level health and sanitation programs. From 1963 to 1968, he lived in New Delhi, India, where he served as a Ford Foundation consultant and advisor to the director of the Indian government's Institute of Public Health Administration and Education, assisting with the development and administration of an extensive family planning and health program in each of India's states. Included in the institute's operation was a staff-training program for senior administrative personnel, for which Leavell assumed major responsibility.

In the autumn of 1968 at the request of the World Health Organization Hugh Leavell undertook a review of the concept of regionalization of health services. His report to WHO reveals the depth of his understanding of the administrative process and his respect for the role of health administrators. He spoke of the importance of knowledge and skills and of values such as the courage to "fight hard for changes in the right direction and oppose strongly those that would move in the wrong direction." He saw regionalization as a rational and efficient way of organizing health services to ensure their optimal utilization and called upon WHO to support evaluative studies of regionalized health services in different parts of the world.

Leavell's research skills were focused more on raising significant questions related to the organization, administration, and operation of community health programs and on stimulating and guiding multidisciplinary teams to obtain answers than on carrying out the research himself. He worked tirelessly in securing funds for the research programs in his department and in assisting his staff with critical insightful analysis of their research problems.

Leavell's publications reflect his professional philosophy and practice. One of his earliest works was a monograph on *Teaching Preventive Medicine to Medical Students* published by the Commonwealth Fund in 1941. Perhaps most of his students and colleagues would consider his major work to be his *Textbook of Preventive Medicine for the Doctor in His Community*, published in several editions by McGraw-Hill. A large number of articles in a variety of scientific journals address his wide-ranging interests in the team concept, the role of the social sciences in medicine and public health, administrative problems, curriculum concerns in schools of public health, and community relationships.

The singular professional qualifications and accomplishments already described were patently enhanced by Leavell's personal qualities. He was compassionate, sensitive, gracious, courteous, thoughtful, warm and friendly, dignified, genuinely concerned about the needs and problems of his staff and students, genteel, quiet, even shy, to a degree unexpected in a man of such high esteem and status. His sense of humor was ready leaven in classroom, faculty session, community meeting, or personal conference. People and their feelings were always of paramount concern to him. He enjoyed social occasions and was a most genial guest and hospitable host.

By any set of standards Hugh Leavell was a giant in the public health domain, one not only several decades ahead of his time but also for the ages.

Gerald Caplan	Isabelle Valadian
Robert Reed	Alonzo Yerby
Elizabeth Rice	Marjorie Young, *Chairman*

Memorial Minute
Faculty of Public Health
February 17, 1977

THEORETICAL PHYSICIST

"Founder of the modern theory of magnetism"

JOHN HASBROUCK VAN VLECK

March 13, 1899 - October 27, 1980

John Hasbrouck Van Vleck, the founder of the modern theory of magnetism, was a pioneer in the development of the quantum theory of matter. His applications of quantum mechanics changed physics and chemistry, deepening our understanding of atomic systems from single molecules to crystalline solids.

Van Vleck was born in Middletown, Connecticut. His father, Edward Burr Van Vleck, was then professor of mathematics at Wesleyan College, where since 1853 his grandfather, John Monroe Van Vleck, had been professor of astronomy and mathematics. In 1906 E.B. Van Vleck moved to the University of Wisconsin to begin a long and illustrious career as professor of mathematics.

So it was in Madison that the young John Van Vleck grew up—intending, as he recalled, not to become a college professor and choosing physics as a major because fewer courses were required. Nevertheless, with his A.B. from Wisconsin, Van (as he became known to practically everyone) entered the Harvard Graduate School in February, 1920. His destiny soon became manifest. He received his PH.D. in 1922 and one year later he went to the University of Minnesota as assistant professor of physics.

In 1928 with Abigail Pearson Van Vleck whom he had met and married in Minnesota, Van returned to Wisconsin as professor of theoretical physics. In 1934 Van again left Wisconsin for Harvard to take up a joint appointment in physics and mathematics. He was associated with both departments for several years. He was professor of mathematical physics from 1935 until 1951 and then, until his retirement in 1969, Hollis Professor of Mathematics and Natural Philosophy.

In 1921 Van Vleck began his doctoral research with Edwin C. Kemble, Harvard's first theoretical physicist and one of very few Americans concerned with the deepening crisis in quantum theory. With John Slater as another graduate student and with postdoctoral students like Gregory Breit and Robert Mulliken, Harvard was to become in those years the most active center of quantum theory in this country.

Just five years later Van Vleck, then at Minnesota, was finishing his first book, *Quantum Principles and Line Spectra*, when the discovery of the new quantum mechanics by Heisenberg, Schroedinger, and Dirac revolutionized theoretical physics. His book, a masterful summary of quantum physics to that moment, was rendered partially obsolete, but his efforts were not wasted. Van had laid a broad foundation for the application of the new theory, whose explanatory power he recognized at once.

Soon he was teaching at Minnesota the matrix mechanics of Heisenberg and, along with others in the forefront of the revolution, resolving puzzles of long standing. One of these concerned the dielectric constant of diatomic molecules. It was solved simultaneously, and independently, by Van Vleck and by three European physicists.

Next, he scored a clear first in molecular magnetism—a field he was soon to make his own—by explaining the baffling paramagnetism of nitric oxide. Already in 1930 Van Vleck could attend the memorable Solvay Congress

on Magnetism in Brussels as a leading theorist along with
· Wolfgang Pauli and H.A. Kramers.

Van Vleck's influential book, *The Theory of Electric and
Magnetic Susceptibilities*, was published in 1932. It included
trailblazing treatments of concepts central to condensed
matter physics, a field that now engages more physicists
than any other. It was also a timely textbook, treasured
by many for the unsurpassed lucidity of Van's exposition
of quantum mechanics. No book in modern physics has
had a longer useful life. Even today, it requires
no corrections.

During the next decade Van wrote some 40 significant
research papers—on the structure of molecules, the
quantum theory of valence, atomic states within crystals,
paramagnetism, ferromagnetism, and antiferromagne-
tism. About half of them appeared in the new *Journal of
Chemical Physics*, beginning with its first volume in 1933.
Many decisively influenced subsequent developments in
theoretical chemistry. Within physics in those years,
Van's work was most keenly appreciated in the world's
leading low-temperature laboratories, at Oxford and
Leiden, where progress toward absolute zero depended
on an understanding of the magnetic properties of atoms
embedded in crystalline electric fields.

During World War II Van Vleck headed the theoretical
group at the Radio Research Laboratory at Harvard,
which had been organized to develop countermeasures to
radar. He served at the same time as consultant to the
Radiation Laboratory at the Massachusetts Institute of
Technology, the center of radar development, and to the
Harvard Underwater Sound Laboratory. In these ephem-
eral organizations Van made what proved to be lasting
scientific contributions. A Radio Research Laboratory
report on randomly fluctuating signals became, when
eventually declassified, part of modern communication
theory and a practical aid to radioastronomy. At the
Radiation Laboratory where the absorption of certain cen-
timeter waves in the atmosphere raised unexpected difficulties, Van's understanding of molecular spectra provided

the key to the problem. In retrospect this episode marks the beginning of microwave spectroscopy, a field ready for spectacular growth as soon as postwar laboratories could acquire the new microwave apparatus, and one which Van Vleck's theoretical work would continue to illuminate.

Magnetic resonance was another branch of experimental physics that blossomed after the war. Its central problems concerning line shape and relaxation processes seemed made for the Van Vleck treatment. Building on the foundation he had laid in the 1930s, Van now produced not only the new theoretical tools that were needed, but the physical insight that unified phenomena ranging from nuclear magnetism to ferromagnetism. His last research paper dealing with magnetism was published just 50 years after his first.

Van managed to combine his unflagging scientific productivity with important administrative services to Harvard. As chairman of the physics department in the critical years 1945 to 1949, he was responsible, more than anyone else, for the appointments that were to determine the course of physics at Harvard in the postwar decades. In 1951 Van was persuaded by President Conant and Dean Paul Buck to become dean of the newly formed Division of Engineering and Applied Physics. It was a formidable task. There was controversy both within the faculty and among the alumni of the former Graduate School of Engineering over future directions and the degree to which different areas of modern science, potentially important to technology, should be represented in the division. Van won the respect of all parties. Under his quiet but effective leadership from 1951 to 1957, bridges were constructed—literally and figuratively—between pure scientists, applied scientists, and engineers.

Van received many honors. He was a foreign member of the Royal Society of London, and of the academies of science of France, Sweden, and the Netherlands. He was Lorentz Professor at Leiden in 1960, and Eastman Professor at Oxford in 1961. His honorary degrees include doctorates from Wisconsin, Oxford, Paris, and Harvard. He received the National Medal of Science in 1966, the Lorentz Medal of the Royal Netherlands Academy of Arts and Sciences in 1974. In 1977 he was awarded the Nobel Prize for physics, sharing it with his former student Philip Anderson, and with Sir Nevill Mott.

No list of achievements and honors can reveal the character of this genial man, or explain the admiration and affection felt for him by generations of students and colleagues. Personally unassuming, he was extraordinarily generous with credit to others. His lively wit was exercised gently. He was a never failing source of encouragement and kindness. Van had diverse cultural interests—in music, in art, and in literature—and certain intense loyalties. His loyalty to Harvard was especially strong. So was his devotion to the University of Wisconsin, where he had written his great book and where, not so many years earlier, he had spent his happy undergraduate days. Van's lifelong enthusiasm for railroad transportation, and his encyclopedic knowledge of that and other modes of travel were legendary. Van took much pleasure in travel and, with Abigail his constant companion, was at home in many distant places. France and the Netherlands were particularly close to his heart. In all centers of learning, he was welcomed as a great scientist and a warm friend.

Harvey Brooks   Paul C. Martin
Sidney R. Coleman   Robert V. Pound
Edward M. Purcell, *Chairman*

Memorial Minute
Faculty of Arts and Sciences
November 15, 1983

ARCHITECT

"Unity in the arts of design"

WALTER GROPIUS

May 18, 1883 - July 5, 1969

By the end of 1936, students and faculty of the Graduate School of Design knew that Walter Gropius would come to Harvard. In December, replying to an alumnus' complaint about the inadequacy of instruction, Dean Joseph Hudnut noted the imminent arrival of "one of the most distinguished of European architects and town planners." During that month, Hudnut had written in the *American Architect* of his agreement with Walter Gropius' viewpoints and concerns regarding the problems facing the profession.

Gropius' real architectural reputation had begun in 1911 with the Fagus shoelace factory (Alfeld a.d. Leine) which he designed as much for its workers as for its sympathetic owner. His second building of note was built for the German Werkbund Exhibition in Cologne in 1914. He already was at that time a proponent of industrialization in the building industry. The interruption of World War I, in which he served four years in the hussars, hardly inhibited his preoccupation with ideas for education in the design fields. On April 1, 1919, he established the Bauhaus in Weimar. This was a new kind of school, very different from the schools for artists and craftsmen, and from those for industrial workers; in the Bauhaus, he sought comprehensiveness and integration of all of those artistic, craft, and industrial skills. To do so, he had to develop a very special kind of curriculum and train a special kind of teacher. His faculty included Paul Klee, Wassily Kandinsky, Gerhard Marcks, Johannes Itten, László Moholy-Nagy, Josef Albers, Herbert Bayer, and Marcel Breuer, among others.

The removal of the Bauhaus from Weimar to Dessau for political reasons accelerated the development and spread of his influential ideas. The works of his private office were examples of a new honesty in architecture; the new Dessau Bauhaus building would rank as one of the landmarks of modern design. His retirement from the Bauhaus in 1928 gave him greater opportunity for practice and travel until the advent of the Nazis. From 1934 to 1937 in England, Gropius encountered an introspective and austere economic environment; but it was also a socially conscious and searching intellectual one. He was impressed by English restraint and understatement. He carried out few projects in England. Though these were significant in their influence on contemporary architecture, they hardly suggested what would be the magnitude and qualities of his contributions to the United States and the world from 1937 on.

Within a month of Gropius' arrival in Cambridge in April 1937, the *Architectural Record Magazine* published his views on architectural education. Disclaiming his ability to discuss the subject in detail without having had experience in the United States, Gropius expressed his desire to develop within each young potential architect the ability to approach a problem according to its technical, economic, and social conditions.

The *American Architect and Architecture Magazine* in May 1937 stated that his "coming to Harvard gave additional emphasis to the fact that the United States is on the way to being the Mecca for architectural education."

Although architecture in the United States had produced its share of pioneers, architectural education remained patterned on the system of the École des Beaux Arts. The new architectural thought and the new educational directions which had developed in Europe during the early decades of the twentieth century had made scarcely any impact in the United States. At Harvard University, Gropius found a strange mixture of a 300-year established custom and yet a fierce independence of thought. Hudnut already had relegated the Classic to its place in history; yet, Beaux Arts attitudes remained little changed in the reorganized Graduate School of Design.

Gropius brought to Harvard an articulate statement of the new movement in architecture with its focus on social values and its emphasis on rational means of construction. Initially, only within the confines of Gropius' studio would change be obvious. Rapidly, it permeated the other classes and when he was appointed chairman of the Department of Architecture in 1938, the Beaux Arts approach to architecture was truly of the past. Subsequently, virtually all the schools in the United States would turn away from the Beaux Arts system and adopt curricula based on the new attitudes and principles.

At Harvard, Gropius faithfully appeared twice each week at each student's drafting-table; his comments attracted surrounding students who most frequently benefited much more than the nervous individual presenting sketches for criticisms. His demeanor quiet, his words few, and his sketches still fewer, Gropius, nevertheless, elicited response from every student. A gesture, a line from a stubby pencil out of his vest-pocket, or a few questions were sufficient to give a new direction, or to make one abandon all of an earlier effort and to take a fresh approach. His dedication was complete; following full days of departmental administration including four or five hours of studio criticism, he frequently said, "I feel like a disemboweled chicken!"

On many occasions, he appealed to his entire class to concern itself with the realities of the housing problem and the requirements of the then emerging legislation, to examine the earlier experience, and to experiment in construction methods. He emphasized the need to seek and to try to understand the responsibilities of the architect toward the social problems then seen in the sharp exaggeration of the Depression; in this he would reiterate constantly his view of the relatedness of ideas and actions to the totality of the environment. He spoke of the complexity of society and the need for collaborative effort to solve its problems. He challenged each student to find within himself his own expression, his own interpretation—frequently within a team or collaborative effort of architects, city planners and landscape architects. Always, Gropius called for diversity within unity.

Gropius was always in superb control of himself. Sometimes a perturbed reaction was revealed by the finger-twisting of his right eyebrow, an even more careful search for appropriate words, then to be expressed in accents much influenced by his stay in England. His restraint and economy of words was offset by sudden opportunities in which he revealed himself, his doubts, and his convictions. His charisma was extraordinary and the warmth of regard in which Gropius was held by former students, friends and colleagues was a lasting one.

Though Gropius preferred to be known as an architect, he became a symbol of education to the public. This identification was already twenty years old in 1937; then he wrote in an article, "Education of Architects and Designers":

> It is not so much ready-made dogma that I want to teach, but an attitude toward the problems of our generation which is unbiased, original and elastic.

At Harvard, he was able to complete the changes in education in architecture and related design fields which he had begun in the Bauhaus. Despite the constant trend toward specialization, Gropius remained firm in his view that comprehensive education must precede narrower concentration. Gropius was determined that there would

150

be no mold, no initiation, but within each student the development of his own personality, direction, and approach; one need only look at the work of some of his students whose names are familiar: Herbert Bayer, Marcel Breuer, I.M. Pei, Paul Rudolph, Victor Lundy, Ernest Kump, or Edward Barnes.

Some 80 percent of his Harvard students have been teachers in design fields; so have more than 70 percent of the Bauhauslers. Gropius said, "In assessing the potential and contribution of a teacher, I ask, 'Does the man live what he teaches?' This must be the strength."

His appointment at Harvard, under the custom prevailing in some of the professional graduate schools, permitted and encouraged private practice. Deterred by the Depression as much as by the fact that Gropius and Marcel Breuer were unknown, commissions for work came slowly to their small office in College House, Harvard Square. Despite his new-won competence in the English language, his well-known democratic principles and actions, and his acceptance by neighbors and colleagues, the prewar years and the period of the war itself made him conscious that he was an alien—a citizen of an aggressor nation with which his host country was at war—though he became a U.S. citizen in 1944.

Soon after his arrival in the U.S., Gropius concerned himself with the problems of lowering housing costs. Calling for reorganization of the construction industry better to meet the problems of a new world beyond the war through industrialization, his teachings and writings were directed toward the role and responsibilities of the architect in such a program.

Immediately after the war, he renewed his Chicago ventures which had begun when he and Adolf Meyer entered the *Chicago Tribune* competition in 1922; his first postwar activity was his involvement in Michael Reese Hospital's and the South Side's pioneering efforts in planning, redevelopment and conservation. In 1947, he was advisor to General Lucius Clay on the reconstruction of Germany; and in 1949 he was given his initial opportunity to build for Harvard: the Harkness Commons and the Graduate Center.

Despite his impatience to resume full-time practice, Gropius, as requested by President Conant, had agreed to continue teaching at Harvard beyond the usual retirement age. In midsummer 1952, in his seventieth year, Gropius announced his retirement. At an age when most men retire to rest on past accumulations of wealth and prestige, Gropius began his emeritus career in full vitality and with enthusiasm. He hoped to spend his time, not in philosophic retrospection, but in pursuit of an expanded architectural and planning practice. Yet, immediately, President Conant sought his advice in respect to the School of Design. Though he had recommended his successor and dean of the Graduate School of Design, he sincerely hoped that he would not find it necessary to exercise "the hand of a dead chairman," an expression which frequently he used to refuse requests for his intervention in matters of school administration and policy. Unfortunately, peace of mind was not within the legacy of his emeritus position. Ten years after his retirement, Gropius was persuaded to become a member of the Overseers' Visiting Committee for the Graduate School of Design. Though solicited for counsel by dissenting factions or individual faculty members, Gropius maintained, outwardly at least, a stoic calmness, perhaps to conceal his real involvement and concerns with the threat of fragmentation and divisiveness in the school.

International honors and recognition came in a steady stream: among these, more than three score honorary degrees, memberships (such as that in Phi Beta Kappa), prizes, and gold medals, including those of the American Institute of Architects and the Royal Institute of British Architects, as well as the Albert Medal of the Royal Society of Arts, Germany's coveted Grand Cross of Merit and Goethe prizes, were his. Perhaps none pleased him so much as the honorary degree awarded by Harvard. In June, 1953, he wrote to an alumnus:

The Harvard Commencement Day last week, at which I got an honorary degree as Doctor of Arts, was quite impressive. I felt like entering the Garden of the Gods. The Harvard people certainly know how to make it a real honor if they want to honor somebody.

The next sixteen years were productive ones. His practice with TAC (The Architects Collaborative) became worldwide and epitomized a process of teamwork. Among his works are the Pan Am Building, New York; the Athens Embassy; the Federal Building, Boston; the University of Baghdad; town planning, Selb, Bavaria; and housing for 35,000 families in southeast Berlin—named in his honor "Gropiusstadt." Now there was time for travel and in visits everywhere he was received as a conquering hero. Lectures, articles, and books were fewer but painstakingly prepared. The first of his books was *The New Architecture and the Bauhaus* and the last *Apollo in the Democracy.*

A man whose extraordinary vigor and horsemanship rivaled that of Cicero's nonagenarian King Masinissa of Numidia, Gropius rode three hours each day during his annual vacation in Arizona in March 1969. He was working full days and weeks in his architectural office in May. Despite his years, his death on July 5, 1969, was, as in the instances of Frank Lloyd Wright and Le Corbusier, a premature one for the profession and for the world.

Ronald Gourley   Edward K. True
Huson T. Jackson   Wilhelm V. von Moltke
Caroline Shillaber   Reginald R. Isaacs, *Chairman*

Memorial Minute
Faculty of Design
October 10, 1969

HEALTH ENGINEER

*"Innovator in industrial medicine, remembered
for the iron lung"*

PHILIP DRINKER

December 12, 1894 - October 19, 1972

Philip Drinker became a
member of the Faculty of Public
Health in 1921 and helped
create the first industrial hygiene
department in any academic
institution. In 1936, he became
professor and department head
and served in this capacity until
his retirement in 1961, completing 40 years on the Harvard

University faculty. His professional career coincided
almost exactly with the principal period of innovation
and discovery in the history of industrial hygiene, and
he made many original contributions to this discipline.
During this period, he taught and profoundly inspired
two generations of students of industrial hygiene and,
through them, his influence spread worldwide.

Philip Drinker was graduated from Princeton in 1915
with a degree in chemistry and from Lehigh in 1917 with
a degree in chemical engineering. Following World War
I service in the Air Force, he held a number of industrial
engineering assignments until he joined his brother
Cecil, a physiologist, at the then new School of Public

Health at Harvard to work on the development of devices "for determining dust and methods for appraising the healthiness of working conditions in mines, factories, and the like," an early recognition that the engineering aspects of industrial medicine deserved major attention. Among the earliest efforts were studies designed to develop tables of permissible concentrations of air contaminants for daily working exposures in industry. This activity continued under the auspices of the American Conference of Governmental Industrial Hygienists and became a major factor in the maintenance of safe working conditions.

Combining courage with scientific curiosity and concern for worker's health, Drinker was a willing "guinea pig" in his own studies as well as those of others. He cheerfully exposed himself to metals that are known to produce metal fume fever, intoxicating solvents, and the inhalation of countless mineral dusts of then unknown toxicity. He was convinced that whatever was unacceptable in the laboratory was intolerable in industrial practice and he exercised his engineering ingenuity to devise control methods that would be effective without the intervention of the worker.

Drinker's career at Harvard encompassed a long and fruitful collaboration with his brother and with other physicians associated with the Harvard Medical School and its teaching hospitals in the application of engineering to medical problems of a diverse nature. An investigation which began as an effort to develop better methods of resuscitating victims of electric shock and illuminating gas poisoning resulted in the invention with Louis Shaw, of the iron lung, a device that induced artificial respiration and maintained the life of those suffering respiratory paralysis, principally from poliomyelitis. It is difficult for those brought up in the era of the Salk and Sabin vaccines to imagine the terror and suffering formerly evoked by the annual visitations of polio. The outpouring of gratitude and honors that followed the development of the Drinker respirator by the collaborative efforts of physician and engineer recognized the fulfillment of an urgent need and resulted in the conferring of many honors, including the John Scott Medal of the City of Philadelphia and honorary doctorates from Norwich University in 1940 and Hahnemann Medical College in 1942.

Other widely recognized engineering contributions to clinical and occupational medicine were his proposals for the first air-conditioned wards for the treatment of premature infants that were placed in operation in 1925 and have remained unchanged in principle and for the use of helium-air mixtures for deep diving which made possible the dramatic escape of the crew of the disabled submarine, USS *Squalus*, in 1939. In the field of occupational health, Philip Drinker's interests in the physiology of respiration and worker health resulted in the development of many new protective devices such as dust and fume masks.

Drinker organized a New England Seminar for Industrial Hygiene in 1935. This proved so successful that others followed in New England and elsewhere and stimulated the founding in 1939 of the American Industrial Hygiene Association, which elected him president in 1942 and conferred upon him the Cummings Memorial Award in 1950.

During World War II, Philip Drinker served his country as director of industrial health for the U.S. Maritime Commission and U.S. Navy Contract Shipyards and in this assignment trained a high percentage of the postwar leaders in the occupational health professions. After the war, he was a Fulbright visiting professor at Queen's University, Belfast, and lectured on engineering and industrial hygiene.

Soon after its establishment, the U.S. Atomic Energy Commission engaged his services as a consultant on health and safety matters. Rapidly, this responsibility extended outward to the protection of populations beyond the gates of the nuclear energy installations and stimulated a new research interest that was to develop into an early leadership position in understanding and controlling air pollution.

The *Journal of Industrial Hygiene* was started at Harvard in 1919 by Dean David Edsall, Cecil Drinker, and others as a joint enterprise with American and English co-workers. Initially, the subject matter was mainly industrial surgery and orthopedics, but it became apparent that engineering aspects deserved major attention and, accordingly, Philip Drinker was made assistant editor soon after his arrival at Harvard. He became editor-in-chief in 1936 and continued in this post until 1949 when the *Journal of Industrial Hygiene* merged with *Occupational Medicine*, an American Medical Association journal, to form the *Archives of Industrial Hygiene and Occupational Medicine*. Editorship of the combined journals remained with Professor Drinker until his retirement in 1961. He was a prolific and adept writer and produced scores of articles on subjects associated with his extensive laboratory research and his many occupational disease control studies in industry. With W.I. Clark he wrote a textbook entitled *Industrial Medicine* and with T. Hatch a textbook entitled *Industrial Dust* which, in two editions, has been an industrial hygiene classic for decades.

As *Journal* editor, Professor Drinker maintained a close relationship and a vigorous correspondence with fellow professionals throughout the world. His British colleagues promptly reported their observations regarding the disastrous 1952 London smog episode and asked for his advice. Fortuitously, he was at that time investigating permissible concentrations of sulfuric acid mist for workmen in the smelting industries, and the London experience stimulated him to initiate a new research program designed to investigate the toxic effects of much lower concentrations of sulfuric acid mist and sulfur dioxide, thought to be the principle toxic agents in the London smog fatalities. From the beginning, the results have figured prominently in the formulation of U.S. air quality standards for sulfur oxides and have contributed importantly to worldwide understanding of the manner in which air pollutants affect human health. He was honored for his contributions to the understanding and control of air pollution by being invited to present the 1956 Harben Lectures of the British Royal Institute of Public Health and Hygiene.

A person of public acclaim and surpassing professional reputation, Philip Drinker was universally liked and respected. He was a man of staunch principles, with an uncommon amount of common sense, without a suggestion of guile or arrogance. He was as ready to acknowledge in booming tones his own errors as to point out those of his friends and colleagues, the latter always with kindness and usually with humor. Those who knew him well, after giving him his full due as an outstanding pioneer and innovator in his chosen profession, cherish most the memory of him as a friend and a man of extraordinary character. He was a poised and skillful teacher. Although some of his students were engineers and others were physicians, he had the notable ability to address each in ways appropriate to his special interests. His lectures were fashioned not only to the needs of a diverse student body, but also to the distinctive response of each new class.

In retrospect, the most important scientific contribution of Philip Drinker may have been his demonstration of the enormous benefits that can accrue from close collaboration between engineer and physician. Between Philip and his brother, Cecil, the fields of applied physiology and industrial hygiene were barely distinguishable, and their teaching and research reflected this fruitful interdisciplinary collaboration. His work with outstanding physicians, including Louis Shaw and Kenneth Blackfan, during his active years at Harvard provide notable evidence of the potential of interdisciplinary research in many problems of preventive and clinical medicine, including the entire field of environmental health, which may be thought of as an enlargement of Philip Drinker's lifelong concerns. The close collaboration with physicians which Philip Drinker cultivated has matured through the years into the new discipline called bioengineering.

William A. Burgess   James L. Whittenberger
Harold A. Thomas, Jr.   Melvin W. First, *Chairman*

Memorial Minute
Faculty of Public Health
May 17, 1973

VI. Art and Healing

ALGEBRAIST

"Penetrating insight, first-rate craftsmanship"
RICHARD DAGOBERT BRAUER
February 10, 1901 - April 17, 1977

Richard Dagobert Brauer, one of the great algebraists of our century, was born in Berlin, received his PH.D. from the University of Berlin and accepted his first position as Privatdozent at Königsberg. He emigrated to the United States with his family in 1933. After spending a year at the University of Kentucky,  he went to the Institute for Advanced Study at Princeton to spend one year as assistant to Hermann Weyl. Of this Weyl wrote:

> It was the happiest experience in scientific collaboration I ever had in my life. It was wonderful to observe with what sure, deft and delicate hands he managed his algebraic problems. Penetrating insight combined with first-rate craftsmanship.

In 1935, after his sojourn at the Institute for Advanced Study, Brauer went to Canada and spent 13 years at the University of Toronto. He then moved to the University of Michigan, and stayed there for three years. Brauer's affiliation with Harvard began in 1951, and lasted for the rest of his career. Life in Boston suited him both mathematically and personally. He was of a sociable disposition. It was not unusual for him to invite his mathematics class to a party at his house in Belmont. For his classes, for the more personal kind of teaching, for his graduate research students, he had, and displayed, undiluted love. He had an exceptionally large number of students, and from among them made many of his close lifetime friends.

Brauer's dissertation was written under the direction of Issai Schur. Schur had been the pupil of Frobenius, and was the principal early developer of the theory of group representations, which Frobenius had invented at the end of the nineteenth century. Brauer was to spend much of his life enriching this theory, and augmenting it with one of his great contributions: the theory of modular characters. This latter theory has been the key to many vaults and promises to continue to be so.

With regard to Brauer's sustained effort of two decades and his ultimate assault on the famous conjecture of Schur, Weyl once wrote that he was especially struck by

> the steadiness in the flow of his ideas, and the steadiness of his growth. Step by step, the problems which he attacks increase in importance and depth. . . . What a way from his thesis to this achievement [Schur's conjecture] by which he crowned his systematic investigation of modular representations! and what a harvest he brought on his way!

The remaining 32 years of Brauer's life were indeed graced by a continued "readiness in the flow of his ideas." He was a pioneer in the program of classifying the finite simple groups, and remained one of the important contributors to the field up to his death. When he retired in 1958 from the presidency of the American Mathematical Society he suggested in the address he gave at that occasion that he had reached the time in life when a mathematician "disappears into anonymity." In retrospect, it is striking how inapplicable this phrase is to Brauer.

Three years later, one of the most celebrated victories of group theory occurred: Feit and Thompson succeeded in proving the "solvability of all groups of odd order"; the proof being astonishing for both its complexity and its length (over 300 pages). Feit, in discussing this proof in his 1970 address at the International Congress of Mathematicians in Nice, gave Brauer credit for taking the first critical step which made it possible. The Feit-Thompson proof opened the door to the long-sought goal of classifying the finite simple groups. The last 15 years of Brauer's life witnessed a tremendous burst of activity directed towards its achievement, and Brauer's work during this period was of fundamental importance to this endeavor. Nor did it ever let up. Brauer's colleagues in group theory tell us that, going through his papers after his death, they found six essentially complete manuscripts, ready for submission for publication, containing new ideas relevant to this program. Brauer's professional interests were concentrated in algebra and especially group theory. Nevertheless, all students of number theory are familiar with some of his notable successes in that subject and the concept of the "Brauer group" has found its uses in diverse branches of mathematics. Brauer received many honors: the American Mathematical Society Cole Prize (1949); the National Medal for Scientific Merit (1971); and several honorary degrees.

Brauer clearly demanded much of himself in his work, and at the same time was sympathetic with the struggles of others; not only those of great, but also those of more modest promise. He had no patience with people who assumed postures of importance.

John T. Tate   George W. Mackey
              Barry C. Mazur, *Chairman*

Memorial Minute
Faculty of Arts and Sciences
December 11, 1979

NOBEL LAUREATE

"Profound achievement in human biology"

JOHN FRANKLIN ENDERS

February 10, 1897 - September 8, 1985

John Enders' stature as a scientist should not be remembered or assessed merely by the
vast array of honors which were
bestowed upon him—including
the 1954 Nobel Prize, the Presidential Medal of Freedom in
1963, the Cameron Prize of
University of Edinburgh, a
Lasker Award, the Ricketts
Award of University of Chicago, the Robert Koch
Médaille, the Galen Medal of the London Society of
Apothecaries, the Passano Award, the Kimble Methodology Research Award, the Charles V. Chapin Medal, the
Gordon Wilson Medal, the R.E. Dyer Lectureship
Award, the Diesel Médaille; memberships in the National
Academy of Sciences, the Royal Society (London), and
the French Academy of Sciences; honorary degrees from,
among others, Yale, Harvard, Trinity College, North-
western, Jefferson Medical College, Western Reserve,
Tulane, Tufts, Hartford, Duke, University of Pennsylvania, University of Ibadan, and Oxford.

Enders' many achievements in human biology were
profound and opened vast areas of research to subsequent

investigators who have followed his guidelines, utilized his techniques, and furthered his concepts.

What must be emphasized for today's (and future) young researchers is that this extraordinary man succeeded while maintaining unwaveringly impeccable standards of personal and scientific honesty. His was a unique style, one which has nearly vanished from biomedical science in the 1980s. The results of his studies were never "published" in press conferences or through other media events. They were presented in fastidiously composed papers submitted to journals with critical editorial review.

Enders did not draft a manuscript until experiments had been repeated over and over again, assuring total reliability and reproducibility. He wrote and rewrote these manuscripts meticulously (in pencil on yellow lined paper) to make them clear, succinct, precise, and thoroughly readable. A demanding philologist, he had pursued graduate studies in English preceding his choice of a career in microbiology. The pathways to exciting results were recorded in so lucid a fashion that an interested reader could recreate the reported experiment in his own laboratory simply by following the "materials and methods" section of an Enders paper.

The openness and generosity of the Enders laboratory were striking. These characteristics stemmed directly from "the Chief" (as most of us called him), who believed that the fruits of research would be most rapidly nurtured by sharing with others who could then conduct the next experiments. The door was always open to visitors from throughout the world. Few scientists left such a visit unaccompanied by carefully packaged boxes containing samples of virus, cells, sera, reagents, or other ingredients, to ensure the ready progress of their own experiments back at home. The data in laboratory notebooks were shared with visitors who sought specific information on experiments recently completed or still underway.

Politics in the laboratory were generally liberal, occasionally radical, but rarely conservative. As Fred Robbins

167

[Frederick C. Robbins, Nobel laureate in medicine, 1954, with Enders and Thomas H. Weller] observed, John Enders with advancing years reversed the usual aging trend by his increasing liberal commitment. In contrast, his economics were stringently conservative, perhaps penurious. The scion of a wealthy Connecticut banking and insurance family, he was scrupulously protective of the taxpayer's dollar, never profligate in his laboratory budget.

For the majority of the many productive years of the Research Division of Infectious Diseases which Enders headed at Children's Hospital, only two modest grants were maintained, one from the Armed Forces Epidemiological Board, the other from the National Institute of Allergy and Infectious Diseases of the National Institutes of Health. It was not unusual for unexpended funds to be returned at the end of a fiscal year. Salaries were modest and any proposed increase for a technician, secretary, or faculty member was scrutinized with Yankee parsimony.

The superficial Enders guise was that of a round-shouldered, overburdened, sometimes meek, pedantic scientist—a caricature he deliberately fostered and exploited effectively as a shield against the unwelcome intrusion of assignments to distracting committee or administrative chores. In fact, he was a strong, competitive, thoroughly contemporary, artful academician who conserved his energies for those challenges he judged worthy.

He traveled infrequently and only on special occasions, either to enjoy a few days with his beloved wife Carol at their seaside home in Waterford, Connecticut, or, rarely, to attend the required meeting of a funding group or a scientific session where topics of particular interest to him would be discussed. With some predictability, an acute respiratory infection often afflicted him the day prior to a scheduled commitment in Washington, D.C., so that one of the junior staff was quickly mobilized to depart for a review session to report on the laboratory's activities. Although it was flattering to be entrusted with

168

such a mission, we also viewed it as our responsibility to protect the Chief so that his research could continue uninterrupted.

Teaching was constant and personal. Every day Enders took time to make the rounds of the laboratory benches to talk with each fellow and ask, "What's new?" That two-word question was a wonderfully effective stimulus to enhanced laboratory productivity because a fresh answer to the inquiry earned extra personal time with the Chief to discuss one's observations. To preserve this intimacy and a full awareness of all projects in the laboratory, he never accepted more than a few trainees and one or two faculty associates at any time.

Formal teaching outside the laboratory was quite another matter. Each year he faithfully made his way to Amphitheater D to participate in the virology sessions of the microbiology course for medical students. His complete lecture was handwritten in advance as painstakingly as scientific manuscripts. They were a joy to read.

Their delivery was another matter. After adjusting the microphone around his neck and checking that it was live, he would extract a large handkerchief from his vest pocket and blow his nose with significant amplification by the sound system. We were never certain whether that was a nervous habit or meant deliberately to arouse the students' attention or laughter, but it usually did both. He extracted a large gold pocket watch from another compartment of his vest and placed it on the lectern to assure punctuality in his presentation. The lecture was articulate, but dry, and rarely overwhelmed the audience. His own disciples sat squirming in the back row seats hoping the students would perceive the gems they were receiving. After the lecture, we joined him for the short walk back to the laboratories in the old Carnegie building of Children's Hospital, assuring him of how fine his presentation had been, even though both he and we suspected that few of the students appreciated what had been offered.

We did animal work in a basement room housing the monkeys with which we studied enteroviruses and later measles and rubella viruses. He greatly enjoyed his visits to the animals accompanied by the fellows who were responsible for those experiments. His own experience had been gained under the tutelage of John Lyons, the redoubtable animal caretaker of the Department of Bacteriology and Immunology. We were the next generation to inherit the Lyons'-Enders' tricks for managing reluctant simians. These included a blend of benevolence and craftiness not unlike the way Enders managed higher primates.

There were other idiosyncracies, some inadvertent and others deliberate. Enders arrived late each morning in the laboratory, chauffeured by Carol and carrying one of a set of wicker baskets in which she had deposited a lovingly prepared jelly sandwich, some fresh fruit, and several pieces of her superb chocolate fudge all neatly wrapped and contained within a fine linen napkin. Unconsumed fudge was the reward of those workers who remained with him late in the day, long after usual departure times. Often while he ate at his desk he read journals, particularly *Science*, in which he relished reviewing the articles outside his own field. Geology, physics, botany, and other topics all fascinated him, and he had the enviable knack of quickly perceiving the main point of each presentation.

Bow ties and vests were a daily uniform, with four-in-hand ties reserved only for special occasions. Atop the shelves in his office was an array of hats of every sort, collected personally or presented by many of his friends and admirers, to be donned when a particularly significant laboratory test was to be examined: a poliovirus neutralization test, a complement-fixation test for antibodies after inoculation of monkeys with an attenuated measles virus, a titration of rubella virus, a review of cell transformation by SV-40. There was an exciting combination of humor, suspense, elegance, and intensity as we gathered round for the occasion.

170

The technicians in the laboratory were "the girls" and the fellows were "the boys" until Drs. Anna Mitus, Martha Leas, and Catherine Wilfert antiquated this nomenclature by their selection as fellows. Nothing was too menial for a fellow. In order to learn thoroughly every detail of cell culture and virology techniques, the fellows shared responsibility with the technicians for the preparation of common pools of media, reagents, and cell cultures.

Before the advent of plastic disposable laboratory ware, there was a glassware preparation room presided over by a succession of autocratic Latvian émigrés who ruled with an iron hand. Even the Chief hesitated to alter their procedures without keen diplomatic negotiations. They were exemplary individuals who made their way in a new country via the glassware room, but evenings and weekends were painter, agronomist, geologist, and Shakespearean actor. Each was treated with the same respect afforded all colleagues in the Enders laboratory, in total accord with the general theme of his approach to humanity. In 12 years of close daily association, I can recall only one person for whom he could not find some redeeming feature, and that man was indeed a rogue.

Like his own mentor, Hans Zinsser, Enders was a man of many talents. He appreciated music and enjoyed playing Bach at home on his piano, but rarely before an audience. At his annual Christmas party, he was a courtly figure in dark trousers, vest, and a crimson smoking jacket as he plied each guest with a treacherous whiskey punch made from his own recipe.

One delightful tradition involved the drawing of names from a hat, a few weeks before the holiday, for the giving of Christmas presents. More attention was focused on the requisite poem which accompanied the gift, and which was read aloud at the time of presentation, than on the gift itself. Some of the efforts were indeed remarkable, but none matched those which Enders himself composed, and it was a true joy to be the recipient of his poem and gift. The evening ended with the Chief at the

171

piano and his guests gathered round him, his "family" singing Christmas carols.

Enders' choice in literature was broad and eclectic, ranging from ancient to modern, Homer to *The Hardy Boys*. No character in a Shakespeare play had escaped his analysis; a choice of these characters frequently formed the basis for comparison to a contemporary figure under discussion.

Fishing was Enders' favorite outdoor hobby; it took him from the waters of Long Island Sound off the shore of his Connecticut home to the salmon rivers of eastern Canada. The latter included an annual pilgrimage to one of the famed salmon streams where his brother belonged to a private fishing club. If the fishing was good, a large wooden crate arrived in the laboratory containing a beautiful salmon packed in ice. The fellows' responsibility was to clean and prepare the salmon steaks, which were then distributed to all members of the laboratory. The Chief's fiscal conservatism was humorously revealed by his estimate of the probable cost of each salmon based on all the expenses of such a trip to New Brunswick.

At the end of each working day, Enders frequently rode home in a taxi, so often that most of the drivers came to know him well. They called for him at the laboratory exit of Children's Hospital, and often questioned him about the progress of his research. One of his favorite stories was of the driver who advised him to keep on trying so that perhaps someday he, like Dr. Salk, would discover something wonderful.

In its customary fashion, Harvard was never precipitous in promotions; Enders remained an instructor for five years, an assistant professor for seven years, and an associate professor for 14 years (including two years after he received the Nobel Prize). He was firmly convinced that the size or magnificence of laboratory surroundings and equipment had little relationship to productivity or success—if anything an inverse relationship.

This belief was fully compatible with the rather spare rooms which housed his laboratory in the old Carnegie

Building. When Dr. Sidney Farber generously offered additional space in the Jimmy Fund building, two modern laboratories and an office befitting the Chief were then added. There were later moves, to a temporary building near the juxtaposition of the Brigham parking lot and the House of the Good Samaritan, and eventually to the research building on Longwood Avenue which now bears his name. He never coveted space, tolerated these moves amicably, and maintained genuine concern that his needs not impede resources for younger investigators. Is it any wonder that those who knew him loved and revered this great and gentle man?

Reminiscence of John Franklin Enders by Samuel Lawrence Katz, M.D. 1952, Wilburt C. Davison Professor and Chairman of the Department of Pediatrics, Duke University Medical School, *Harvard Medical Alumni Bulletin* (Winter 1985). © *Harvard Medical Alumni Bulletin*, reprinted by permission.

SCHOLAR OF ART

"Intuition buttressed by a perceptive eye and a vast storehouse of knowledge"

JAKOB ROSENBERG

September 5, 1883 - April 7, 1980

Jakob Rosenberg's youthful plan to enter his family's art and antiquities business in Berlin was interrupted by the outbreak of the First World War, when he joined a cavalry unit of the German army. In 1915 he was wounded and captured in France, and sent to Scotland. An exchange of war prisoners  brought him to Switzerland where he was free to study art history, first at Bern University and then at Zurich. In Zurich he rented a room, bare as a monk's cell, whose former tenant had left without a word or trace. It was a while before Rosenberg learned that the previous occupant was Lenin, who had boarded a sealed train for the Finland Station. The Soviets later reconstructed the room using every bit of furnishing they could buy from the landlady. Pedantic piety invites error. Rosenberg, whose concern for establishing the correct provenances of objects was professional, maintained that it is his coffee cups, his ash tray, his flower vase that are now enshrined, grossly mislabeled, in the Lenin Museum in Moscow.

174

After the war Rosenberg returned to Germany and apprenticed himself to an art dealer in Munich. He never regretted the experience. In his words: "It helped open my eyes." However, he soon decided that his temperament was ill-suited for the art trade and he resolved to resume his academic studies at Munich University.

Heinrich Wölfflin, then *ordinarius* of art history at Munich, became Rosenberg's teacher. His impact on his student was decisive. Rosenberg's unwavering dedication to a visual rather than a literary approach to art history and to the study of the phenomenon of style was based on Wölfflin's teaching. Although he later rejected some of his professor's oversimplified concepts, he often stressed his fundamental debt to this giant among the founders of modern art history.

Rosenberg received his PH.D. degree summa cum laude from Munich in 1922. His dissertation on Schongauer's drawings was published in the following year. Its topic signaled what was to remain his foremost lifelong interest. In the study of master drawings he made his greatest contribution to connoisseurship.

In 1922 Rosenberg married Elizabeth Husserl, a fellow student at Munich and daughter of Edmund Husserl, the leader of the school of phenomenology in German philosophy. During the course of their long life together he recognized her as one of his most perceptive critics.

After receiving his degree Rosenberg began work in the Berlin print room where he remained until 1935 when he resigned because he found life in a German museum intolerable under the Nazis.

When he joined the Berlin Museum, Wilhelm von Bode was almost 80 years old and still its director-general; Max Friedländer was director of the print room and in his prime. Rosenberg only saw Bode from a distance, but his contact with Friedländer was close. His expertise gained enormously from Friedländer's generous impulse to allow others to share his rich experience. There was much to share. During the course of Rosenberg's years at the print room Friedländer wrote his triumph of connoisseurship, the 14 volumes of *Die altniederländische Malerei.*

Friedländer had proclaimed that connoisseurship was a matter of intuition and he did not believe that analysis of works of art could establish very much. Rosenberg disagreed. He helped demystify connoisseurship by repeatedly demonstrating in his later publications and teaching that what one of its greatest practitioners called a matter of intuition is, in fact, a bit of intuition buttressed by a sharp and perceptive eye, a vast storehouse of historical and technical knowledge, close firsthand familiarity with innumerable works of art, a formidable visual memory, and incessant practice.

After his study years Rosenberg's heart sent him to the seventeenth-century Dutch masters for his specialized research, but never to the exclusion of artists of other schools and periods. His first article appeared in 1925; it was on an unpublished late Rembrandt drawing (Benesch 1036). Seminal studies on Cornelis Vroom and Hobbema quickly followed. In 1928 his classic monograph and catalogue of Jacob van Ruisdael's paintings and drawings was published. He did the lion's share of work on the monumental catalogue of Berlin's Netherlandish drawings, a joint effort of its curators that appeared in 1930. The standard volume on Cranach's paintings that Friedländer and he wrote in collaboration was published in 1932. The revised and enlarged edition of it, which appeared in 1979, was prepared and seen through the press by Rosenberg when an octogenarian.

Rosenberg made notable acquisitions for the Berlin print room while he was its keeper from 1930 until 1935. He also helped save some of its key holdings when he was informed, after the Nazis came to power, that Göring planned to visit the collection to select some choice works by Dürer, Schongauer, and Cranach for what his outrider euphemistically called an extended loan. In preparation for Göring's visit Rosenberg conspicuously displayed an assortment of eighteenth-century French prints depicting themes which cataloguers then categorized as *sujets libres.*

Upon his arrival Göring became so enamored with the exhibited French prints that he made his selection from them, and then happily departed. He never got the Dürers, Schongauers, and Cranachs.

When Rosenberg first visited Harvard in the spring of 1936 his professional reputation was already secure. He was warmly welcomed at the Fogg, and it is not surprising that he found in Paul J. Sachs a kindred spirit because of their shared passion for the graphic arts. At the suggestion of the German medievalist Adolf Goldschmidt, who had taught as a visiting professor at Harvard, and through Paul Sachs's offices, Rosenberg received an invitation to teach in the University's summer school program that year. Rosenberg, who had no experience as a teacher and had done little—if any—lecturing, accepted the challenge, choosing as his subject seventeenth-century Dutch painting. The course was an unqualified success. Indeed, when he returned to Germany at the end of the term, it was with an invitation to return to Cambridge the following year.

In 1937 Rosenberg emigrated to the United States with his wife and their two young children, Wolfgang and Ruth. For the following two years he was research fellow and lecturer in the Department of Fine Arts. An appointment in the Fogg Museum came in 1939 when he was made curator of prints, a post he was to occupy for 25 years. In the following year he was appointed associate professor. He received a permanent appointment at the University as professor in 1948 when he was 55 years old. Harvard awarded him an honorary doctor of arts degree in 1961.

As curator of the Fogg's print department Rosenberg used its modest purchasing funds to expand significantly the range of an already notable collection with selected works of the highest quality by modern and older masters. His expert knowledge and enthusiasm for the graphic arts extended to the art of his own day. Thus, in the 1940s, when works of the German Expressionists, thrown out of German public collections as "degenerate," first began to appear on the market, he secured out-standing examples at rock-bottom prices. He also worked closely with Professor Charles Kuhn, then curator of the Busch-Reisinger Museum, and helped strengthen that museum's remarkable holdings of twentieth-century central European art.

The man who never taught before coming to Harvard became one of the University's most successful and beloved teachers. He did not establish a school but his method of analysis, his concentration on quality, and his keen appreciation of the importance of technical examination for a fuller understanding of works of art left a lasting impression on generations of students. After his retirement, he kept a study in the museum where he received visitors and worked until the last weeks of his life. His callers included students who were eager to make contact with the leading scholar and connoisseur who had known, and now seemed the peer of, Wölfflin, Friedländer, and Frits Lugt. Curators, collectors, and dealers continued to come for his decisive, yet never dogmatic opinions. Some of his most influential teaching was done in these informal meetings.

At the Fogg, Rosenberg became affectionately known as *der heilige Jakob*—not because he was especially devout or of a saintly innocence of the ways of the world. Neither was the case. Other qualities earned him this title. His temperateness was beyond that given to ordinary mortals and even passing experience of the gentleness he radiated was like a laying on of hands. Charity marked his appraisal of people as well as works of art; in judging both he searched for the good before the less good. He was quite capable of sharply adverse judgment—he did not easily suffer fools or fakes—but it was his nature to criticize with uncommon tact, and he could be a supreme master of the art of damning with faint praise.

His scholarly activity never slackened at Harvard. In 1948 his monograph on Rembrandt appeared, the culmination of his long devotion and intense study of Holland's greatest artist. Though the production of books about Rembrandt has become a heavy international industry since his monograph was published more than a generation ago, it remains the most lucid and balanced study of the master's art. Rosenberg's *Great Draughtsmen*, which condenses his enormous knowledge of eight major artists ranging from Pisanello to Picasso, appeared in 1959. His full-dress monograph on Cranach's drawings was published in 1960. He was co-author of the painting section in *Dutch Art and Architecture: 1600-1800* that appeared in the Pelican series in 1966. The following year he published *Quality in Art*, which offers a survey of the criteria of excellence used by earlier critics and a discussion of his own. It is also his credo.

Until the end Rosenberg kept abreast of the scholarly literature and new trends. He recognized that in recent decades technical investigation has made considerable progress and iconographical research has made a contribution to the discipline. But he was skeptical of the efforts now being made to bring safe solutions to often vexing art-historical problems by committee work. For Rosenberg the quality of perception of the individual judge and his direct relationship with the work of art were all-important. The quality of his own perception was perhaps his greatest gift and his direct relationship with works of art could hardly have been closer. They are the constructive and controlling forces of Jakob Rosenberg's writings and the collections he helped form, which will endure as rich sources of pleasure and knowledge for students, scholars, and the wider public.

Marjorie B. Cohn   Sydney J. Freedberg
John P. Coolidge   Ruth S. Magurn
            Seymour Slive, *Chairman*

Memorial Minute
Faculty of Arts and Sciences
March 8, 1983

179

NEUROBIOLOGIST

*"Experimenter and innovator of uncommon
courage and independence"*

STEPHEN WILLIAM KUFFLER

August 24, 1913 - October 11, 1980

Stephen Kuffler's impact on
what is now called neuroscience
could hardly have been predicted, given his early life and
education. Born in Tap, Hungary, he was reared on a small
country estate, where he spent
most of his boyhood riding and
swimming. At the age of 10 he
was sent to a Jesuit boarding
school near Vienna, where he spent the next nine years.
By his own account he was taught religion, Latin, Greek,
and "practically no science." Nevertheless, he entered
medical school in Vienna and graduated in 1937, having
supported himself during these years by tutoring high-
school students in Latin and Greek. As an undergraduate,
pathology was his favorite subject; he had no interest at
all in physiology.

Three months after Kuffler began a residency in
internal medicine in Vienna, the Germans invaded Aus-
tria. Possibly because of his political involvement with
the anti-Nazi group of students, he feared reprisals; in
any case, he left immediately for England, via Hungary

180

and Trieste. Within three months he sailed for Brisbane, Australia. He disembarked in Sydney to look around, and decided to stay. It was now the summer of 1938. In the first few weeks he met Dr. John Eccles, who was looking for a tennis partner. Eccles soon offered Kuffler a junior post in his research laboratory in the Kanamatsu Institute at Sydney Hospital, where he was doing electrophysiological experiments concerned with neuromuscular transmission. By the fall of 1939, they were joined by Bernard Katz, another emigre from Europe; within a few years, the work of Eccles, Kuffler, and Katz became well known throughout the neuroscience community.

Kuffler's first independent discovery was an important one. In 1940, he developed an elegant single nerve-muscle fiber preparation, the first cell-to-cell junction to be studied in isolation. The use of this preparation made an early contribution to the demonstration that neuromuscular transmission is mediated by acetylcholine rather than by ionic current, as Eccles and many others believed. These studies on the nerve-muscle system by Eccles, Katz and Kuffler were precursors of many later investigations in other laboratories on the nerve-muscle system and prepared the way for the subsequent work by Bernard Katz and his colleagues. Almost by accident, Stephen Kuffler had begun a research career that was to last 40 years and range widely over a variety of problems in neurophysiology. He became well known for his ability to choose a new problem, make a decisive and lasting contribution, and then switch to another innovative effort.

When the war ended in 1945, Kuffler, with his wife Phyllis and their first child, Suzanne, left Australia for the United States, where he had obtained a position in the laboratory of Ralph Gerard at the University of Chicago. In 1947, he moved to the Wilmer Institute of Ophthalmology at the Johns Hopkins Medical School. The next 12 years at Hopkins were highly productive, and by the mid-1950s, Kuffler's reputation as one of the leading neurophysiologists in the world was well established.

Between 1948 and 1952, Kuffler, together with C.C. Hunt, carried out a series of experiments on the cat that had an important impact on understanding spinal control of movement and how this is influenced by the gamma-efferent innervation of muscle spindles. Later C. Ezyguirre and Kuffler undertook studies of crustacean stretch receptors, which provided basic information about sensory transduction, as well as synaptic inhibition.

Soon after coming to the Wilmer Institute in 1947, Kuffler turned his attention to the mammalian retina. This interest was stimulated by K. Hartline, his good friend and colleague then in the biophysics department at Johns Hopkins University. Hartline was the first to record the activity of single retinal ganglion cells and stimulate the retina with small spots of light. These studies were done on the frog, and Kuffler carried the work further by making a now-classic study of retinal ganglion cells on the cat. His discovery of the antagonistic center-surround organization of the receptive fields of these cells laid the foundation for the analysis of the central visual pathway carried out by David Hubel and Torsten Wiesel and for other studies of sensory physiology.

At Johns Hopkins Medical School, Kuffler brought together a group of young neurophysiologists who came with him when he moved to the Department of Pharmacology at Harvard Medical School in 1959. This group included Edwin Furshpan, David Hubel, David Potter, and Torsten Wiesel, and they, together with Edward Kravitz, a biochemist who joined the group at Harvard, became members of the Department of Neurobiology, which was created in 1966 with Kuffler as chairman. In establishing this department, he was one of the first to realize that work on the nervous system would be advanced by interdisciplinary research combining anatomy, physiology, biochemistry, and biology. The department quickly became an important training center in neurobiology, and many former students now occupy leading positions in the United States and abroad. In 1974, Kuffler was named the first John Franklin Enders University Professor, and from that time until his death he worked in the laboratory with his characteristic enthusiasm and uncanny instinct for important new areas of research.

As early as 1945, Kuffler and Katz had used the crustacean nerve-muscle preparation as a model for cellular inhibition in higher nervous systems. In the late 1950s and early 1960s, Kuffler returned to invertebrate preparations, and research with several young colleagues, particularly David Potter and Edward Kravitz, led to the demonstration of gamma amino butyric acid (GABA) as the transmitter at inhibitory neuromuscular junctions in these animals. With Josef Dudel, Kuffler provided evidence for the hypothesis that inhibition could be presynaptic as well as postsynaptic, and that GABA mediated presynaptic as well as postsynaptic inhibition. In the 1960s, together with David Potter, John G. Nicholls, and others, he showed that glial cells in the leech are not electrically excitable, but that they are electrically coupled, one of the first demonstrations of this form of communication in cells that do not generate electrical signals. It was shown further that glial cells react passively to the potassium that accumulates in the surrounding narrow clefts as a result of neuronal activity, and might function as a system for buffering the concentration of extracellular ions. Starting in 1970, with another group of postdoctoral fellows (McMahan, Dennis, Harris), he made use of the then-novel Nomarski optics to resolve the outlines of synapses on autonomic neurons in a functionally intact preparation of the frog cardiac ganglion. They provided a clear demonstration of the synaptic localization of acetylcholine receptors on nerve cells and showed that the patterns of acetylcholine sensitivity changed after denervation, just as they do in muscle fibers.

The project upon which Kuffler was engaged at the time of his death was at the forefront of research in synaptic transmission: the role of neuropeptides in the nervous system. Kuffler, with Lilly and Yuh-Nung Jan, had shown that a peptide—luteinizing hormone-releasing hormone (LHRH)—was the excitatory transmitter mediating the slowest of the several synaptic responses in frog sympathetic ganglia. The initial characterization of the postsynaptic mechanisms underlying this peptide-mediated response was just being written up with T. Sejnowski when Kuffler died.

Stephen Kuffler received numerous awards, including the Louisa Gross Horwitz Prize in Biology, the Proctor Award in Ophthalmology, the Dickson Prize in Medicine, the Wakeman Award, the Gerard Prize, the F.O. Schmitt Prize in Neuroscience, and many honorary degrees. He gave the Harvey, Ferrier, and Silliman Lectures, and was a member of numerous societies, among them the American Academy of Arts and Sciences, the Royal Society of London, and the American Philosophical Society.

Kuffler's influence in the neuroscience community was perhaps due almost as much to his personality and character as to his remarkable scientific achievements. A genuinely modest man, he often poked gentle fun at pomposity and pretentiousness, and frequently made jokes at his own expense. In 1964, he was in Bern, Switzerland, where an honorary degree was to be conferred upon him. Before giving his lecture, he went to the men's room, where a man who obviously did not know Kuffler asked if it would be worthwhile to go to the lecture. Kuffler assured him that the lecture was not going to be particularly interesting and said he would be much better off to go home and have dinner with his family. At another solemn occasion attended by important people and speakers, Kuffler was found in the kitchen visiting with the staff. He was known for his puns, and his colleagues tried often, without success, to ration him to one or two a day, but Kuffler's sense of humor remained undeterred and irrepressible.

Very few friends knew that Kuffler, who loved to play tennis, swim, and take vigorous walks, was not in good health during his last 10 years. His diabetes required daily insulin injections, his heart was not strong, his eyes were operated upon for glaucoma. Nevertheless, he never complained; in fact, he seemed to deny his condition himself, insisting upon walking rapidly up the four flights of steps to the laboratory and remaining eager to engage in sports.

Author and co-author of nearly 100 papers, and co-author, with John Nicholls, of the widely used text, *From Neuron to Brain*, Kuffler was primarily recognized as an experimenter and innovator. In contrast to many of his more conservative colleagues, Kuffler had the courage and independence of mind to begin over and over again with an entirely new problem and to develop a preparation (lobster, leech, cat, frog) most likely to provide him with an answer. This approach required uncommon courage and independence of spirit, as most neuroscientists tend to work with one type of preparation and one question in mind. Each of the preparations first developed by Kuffler and his colleagues subsequently became central to the study of important areas of neurobiology.

Thomas L. Benjamin   Edward A. Kravitz
Edwin J. Furshpan   Henry C. Meadow
David H. Hubel   David D. Potter
Eugene P. Kennedy   Torsten N. Wiesel, *Chairman*

Memorial Minute
Faculty of Medicine
January 28, 1983

COMPOSER

"Music that did not succumb to vogues"

WALTER HAMOR PISTON

January 20, 1894 - November 12, 1976

Walter Hamor Piston was born from the family of Pistone, bred as a Piston, and given a berth at Harvard University for nearly 40 years. A prolific composer of eight symphonies, numerous concerti, a cantata and chamber music, including string quartets, quintets, duos, trios, and sonatas, Piston was  the recipient of two Pulitzer prizes, the New York Music Critics Award, and the honorary degree of D.MUS. from Harvard University (1957). He was elected to the National Institute and American Academy of Arts and Letters and the American Academy of Arts and Sciences.

Piston was a pioneer of a musical style which emerged in spite of labels. His was not American music—it was music written by an American. This music did not succumb to the vogues of nationalism, populism, twelve-tone-ism, folkism, or any other "ism" on the horizon, though he assimilated any number of modern techniques. He went his way—a way that had digested the best of the past, tasted the best of the present, and fused it all together for the future. When asked at a New York panel why he didn't write more modern music, he answered,

"It's not my choice really. Every time I write a piece I feel this is going to be new for me and I try to make it new for me—but when I look at what I've written, it's always the same old Piston." That "same old Piston" can be described as spacious music of large proportions which bespeaks a refusal to be hurried, a determination to go where it must go, a feeling for organic growth, coupled with a fine sense of line, chosen sonorities, and a highly disciplined control of feeling. For Piston, "form is the feeling and the feeling is formal."

When it was pointed out to him that there was much understatement in his music, he reminded his critic that he was born in Rockland and summered in Vermont where both peoples "don't say and don't tell." The importance of the position occupied by Piston from 1924 to 1976 is best articulated by Nicholas Slonimsky and Elliott Carter. Slonimsky writes:

> In the constellation of modern American composers, Walter Piston has now reached the stardom of the first magnitude. He has not exploded into stellar prominence like a surprising nova, but took his place inconspicuously, without passing through the inevitable stage of musical exhibitionism or futurist eccentricity.

and Carter writes:

> In the whole field of contemporary music, Walter Piston occupies an important position. He has summed up the tendencies of the past 20 years both here and in Europe and given them broad and masterful expression. Although living in the time of the "lost generation," he found himself in his devotion to music. His unique contribution is to have done this particular work with outstanding excellence in a country where few have ever made a name for themselves as thoroughly craftsmanlike artists. In literature several names come to mind but in music there is hardly one to be found before our time.

"An artist is usually a damned liar" says D.H. Lawrence, "but his art, if it be art, will tell you the truth of his day." Walter Piston's day began in Rockland, Maine, of a typically Down-East family with the exception of paternal grandfather Antonio Pistone. For poor seafaring folk, the idea of a musician in the family was unimaginable. Walter's earliest recollection of sound as music was of his uncle who came to the house, took off his shoes and sang chanteys. When, at the age of seven, Walter began to poke out his uncle's melodies on a piano, his uncle declared, "You'll never have to work for a living." When the family moved to Boston in 1905, Walter's father bought him a violin and his brother a piano. Walter taught himself to play both instruments.

The experience of playing violin in the school orchestra confirmed Walter's love of music, but it was not until he had had training that he was willing to commit himself to it. In the meantime, he learned blacksmithing, mechanical drawing, and machinery at Mechanical High School. After graduation in 1912, he worked for the Boston Elevated as a draftsman. But his heart remained with art and he decided to further his education. The New England Conservatory of Music was too costly, so he opted for art school, which was free. He made his living by performing in restaurants, theaters, and in houses of ill fame—"not so ill in those days, really," he recalled. The music he heard and had to play, however, nearly drove him mad. "It was like saying, I see the cat all the time," he said, "never going so far as to say, I see the *pink* cat." When World War I was declared, he volunteered for the Navy because he liked the sea. He went over to interview the bandmaster at MIT where the band was stationed and realized during the interview that he didn't play a band instrument. After being informed that he would have an audition within a week, he rushed out, bought a saxophone, borrowed an instruction book from the library, and learned to play the instrument overnight. During his audition, he claims not to have played the right notes, but played notes which didn't interfere with what the band was playing. He was accepted but never got off dry land since he was considered too valuable in the music circle. He used his time between rehearsals and performances to learn to play all the other band instruments since they were invariably lying around unused in the rehearsal room. His knowledge existed as part of the experience of the knower. His book on *Orchestration* has sold more than 25,000 copies.

Already married to Kathryn Nason, a painter, Piston, at the age of 26, the "discovery" of "Doc" Davison, entered Harvard as a freshman. The Harvard-Radcliffe Orchestra (Pierian Sodality) can boast of concerts conducted by Piston. In 1924, having graduated summa cum laude, he received the John Knowles Paine Fellowship to study abroad. Nadia Boulanger was the one person he didn't want to study with. "Who wants to go abroad to study with a woman?" After much research, he decided she was the only one to study with.

Piston's decision to continue to teach at Harvard where he was appointed an instructor in 1926 was based both on his love for teaching and on the practical consideration that his musical language produced works for the concert hall of a length that did not bring forth remunerative results. The one and only aspect of academic life that interfered with his composing was his short stint as chairman of the music department, a post which he happily relinquished. As a teacher, he made a deep impression on his students because of his heart, his mind, and his inimitable personality. One could publish a volume of his witticisms. In a fugue class, Piston wrote a subject on the board and marked it *Andante*. One student became agitated and protested that she could not possibly complete a fugue on this subject within a week because she had so much to do. Piston said nothing, but got up and plodded to the blackboard, where he erased *Andante* and substituted *Allegro*.

A long association with the Boston Symphony Orchestra began in the days of Koussevitzky. Piston was a fixture in Symphony Hall, never missing a Saturday night concert. In fact, when he wrote his symphonies, it was with the sound of that orchestra in his inner ear. A wonderful camaraderie existed between Piston and the orchestra.

His sense of brevity and timing produced the following response to Tillman Merritt's declaration that he didn't want the last movement of the Flute Concerto to end after the performance at Symphony Hall. "I guess I'd better add *senza fine*," Piston said.

Piston was gentle but firm with his students. He taught them by innuendo rather than by attack. When a student was at an impasse, he would say "take one note and put another note with it and the first thing you know you have several notes. There's nothing like putting something down to create activity." When people asked him why he spent so much time teaching those classes at Harvard, he would say, "The close contact with the young minds, that's the greatest thing. Without that I don't know where I'd be and sometimes I feel that I learn more from them than they do from me, which they dispute, I'm glad to say. You've got to be right on your toes with those boys. They're right up on what's going on in the world of music and I have to go home and bone up on electronic music and keep at least a week ahead of them." Piston urged his students to try all the things that were being experimented with—getting it out of their systems, before venturing forth on their own. He believed the greatest liberalism on the contemporary scene was that the composer wrote what he wanted to write, and that might even be the triad of C major.

He taught at all levels, the bread-and-butter courses of harmony, counterpoint, fugue, and orchestration. This uninterrupted teaching did not seem unduly to prevent his composition and quite the contrary, it sharpened his abilities to produce his book on *Harmony* as well as his book *On Counterpoint*.

A. Tillman Merritt   Elliot Forbes
Luise Vosgerchian, *Chairman*

Memorial Minute
Faculty of Arts and Sciences
April 10, 1979

PHYSICIAN OF THE HEART

"Unhurried demeanor, unfailing respect for sensitivities"

HERRMAN LUDWIG BLUMGART

July 19, 1895 - March 21, 1977

As an undergraduate at Harvard Herrman Ludwig Blumgart selected courses indicating an interest in psychology and social ethics. In medical school, influenced by Cecil Drinker and Francis Peabody, he became committed to a lifetime in laboratory and clinical research, primarily of the cardiovascular system. His early recognition of the importance of psychological factors in medicine, however, was never lost and was reflected in his teaching of students and in his treatment of patients.

His first scientific publication, in 1922, as a junior author with Drs. Drinker and Peabody was of work done while he was a medical student—*The Effect of Pulmonary Congestion on the Ventilation of the Lung.* His next publication described the first successful clinical application of pituitary extract intranasally in the treatment of diabetes insipidus, based on observations made as a medical house officer at the Brigham.

After completing a Moseley traveling fellowship with Sir Thomas Lewis and Professor Henry Dale in England, he joined the Thorndike Memorial Laboratory in 1924 under Francis Peabody, its first director. During this period he embarked with Otto Yens, a physicist, on a study of the velocity of blood flow in man, utilizing, for the first time in clinical investigation, a radioactive isotope to measure a physiological function. For the next five years, in collaboration with Soma Weiss and others, he carried out classic studies on the velocity of blood flow under conditions of physiological and pharmacological stress as well as in disease states. In recognition of this contribution, the Society of Nuclear Medicine, in 1969, named Dr. Blumgart to its honor roll of nuclear pioneers, the first physician to be so honored.

In 1928, Dr. Blumgart began a lifetime relationship with the Beth Israel Hospital, which had functioned, since 1917, as a nonsectarian institution serving a rapidly enlarging Jewish community. The need for a larger hospital and the hope to establish a medical school affiliation led to the move to its present site on Brookline Avenue. Negotiations with Harvard were successfully completed in February 1928, six months before the new hospital received its first patient. With financial support and research space provided by the hospital, Dean Edsall's concept of a clinical teaching unit was fulfilled, and he advised Dr. Blumgart to accept the hospital's offer of a full-time position as director of medical research with a Harvard appointment as assistant professor of medicine.

At age 33, Dr. Blumgart had undertaken a formidable task. It included the recruitment of a staff to build a strong research department and the development of a teaching program comparable to the older units of the Harvard medical family. Major changes had to be based on Harvard's standards of excellence in teaching and research, but at the same time respecting the sensitivities of the hospital and its supporting community.

During the first year of this program, two fourth-year students came, somewhat reluctantly, for a two-month medical clerkship. They had been transferred from the Brigham by Dr. Henry Christian, who throughout these early years remained ever thoughtful and supportive of his former house officer. Utilizing the judgment and clinical experience of a devoted part-time staff and the special skills of the full-time research group, the medical service within a few years became an exciting center in which teacher, student and patient participated. Though Francis Peabody felt that "the capacity for high-grade research is so rare a quality in itself that it will always be almost impossible to find it combined with the other qualifications demanded of a professor of medicine," Herrman Blumgart and many of his disciples disproved this dichotomy.

In 1936, with the enthusiastic support of Walter Cannon, he inaugurated a series of elective clinics for the first-year students in which he correlated the principles of physiology, and later those of biochemistry and pharmacology, with the problems of patient care. At the beginning of the student's medical careers he emphasized the reliance of clinical medicine on the basic sciences. Later, at Dean Berry's invitation, he began an exercise that became a Harvard tradition—Herrman Blumgart's clinic for the entering class on the very first day. Looking back on this orientation-day clinic, one of his former students remembered his class "being addressed as professional colleagues before we had even opened *Gray's Anatomy* and being led through the mysteries of heart block to the triumph of the pacemaker in one short hour." Many graduates remember this exercise as the most inspiring event in medical school.

His teaching was characterized by an unhurried demeanor, a gentle, soft-voiced manner and an unfailing respect for the sensitivities of the patient. Sitting on the edge of the bed, much to the dismay of his otherwise worshipful nurses, who had laboriously prepared the starched sheets for the chief's rounds, he made it clear to his patients that he cared, and his students and colleagues knew it as well.

As was said of William Harvey, "he practiced medicine with such grace that he seemed to have been born with the skill rather than to have learned it."

On leave of absence from 1943 to 1946 in World War II, he was consultant in the Second Service Command U.S.A. and later in the India-Burma-China theater. His official reports of visits to army medical facilities, ranging from front line dispensaries and receiving stations to hastily renovated government installations, dwelt on the ingenuity and enterprise with which the medical personnel surmounted medical problems under difficult conditions. Recommendations about staffing, equipment, and treatment were couched in terms that were tactful yet calculated to ensure compliance. In his letters home, in spite of his personal hardships, the difficulties of travel, climate and food, he spoke of the joy derived from his medical encounters. Once he entered the hospital wards and made contact with his medical conferees and patients he was on familiar ground. The circumstances were perhaps different, strange and exotic, but the principles were the same. The patient remained the focus of interest.

Shortly after his return from active duty in 1946, he was appointed physician-in-chief at the Beth Israel Hospital and professor of medicine at the Medical School. He played a critical role in the growth of the hospital's research program during the postwar period when the unprecedented availability of private and federal funding made possible great increases in scientific knowledge and major technological advances. To those who felt that this expansion was producing "a robot generation of milli-equivalent practitioners in whom the milk of human kindness had become curdled by molecular biology," he pointed out that "without scientific knowledge a compassionate wish to serve mankind's health is meaningless and it should be possible to acknowledge the triumphs of medicine without denigrating the art."

His abiding interest in psychiatry and the wartime experience in which many of the psychogenic disturbances in soldiers were unresponsive to current organic treatment led him to strengthen the Department of Psychiatry at the hospital and to induce Dr. Grete Bibring to become its head. His understanding and unobtrusive support of this facility in a general hospital offered physicians with their basic science orientation an acceptable theory of personality that they could use with confidence in the psychological management of their patients.

In 1958, he returned to India as visiting professor of medicine under the auspices of the Rockefeller Foundation to help inaugurate a medical residency program at the King George Medical College in Lucknow. Accompanied by his wife, Margaret, he visited many of the places she had first heard about from his wartime letters. He renewed many of the friendships forged during the war and established an unofficial postgraduate training program that brought some of India's most promising students to Boston and the Beth Israel. Their clinical and research experiences in this country helped many to assume leading positions in India's medical institutions.

Blumgart's administrative duties at the hospital and medical school, with responsibilities for teaching, research and patient care, exacted an ever-increasing toll which his youthful appearance, erect posture and cheerful manner belied. His summer home on the shores of Lake Kezar in Maine provided some respite on occasional weekends and during the summer. Although not entirely free from his responsibilities, here he could catch up with his reading, writing, and reviewing manuscripts for publication. He loved to fish for bass in Maine during the summer and for tarpon, snook, and redfish on his winter holiday in the Florida Everglades. Dressed in his grubbiest clothes, with his pockets full of assorted candies to help while away the intervals between strikes, he would set out in the early morning with ordinary light fishing tackle. He was not a fly fisherman and not even an outstanding caster. His choice of equipment and his use of live bait, lures, and spinning rods would not satisfy the purist. Once he was hooked into a fish, all small talk and banter stopped abruptly. He fished with the same intensity and concentration with which he addressed a clinical problem in medicine. If he failed to boat his fish, an immediate postmortem was held in which the guides were confronted with his question, "What did I do wrong?" His companions were often more skillful and equipped with better rods and reels but he invariably ended up with the largest and the greatest number of fish under the most dramatic circumstances.

He was devoted to chamber music and took special pride in listening to his wife, an accomplished pianist, play their favorite Bach, Beethoven, Brahms, and Schubert. Throughout his life, she was his greatest source of renewal and understanding support. She made their home a gracious center for friends and for successive generations of students, residents, and foreign visitors.

When he reached emeritus status in 1962, the occasion was marked by many tributes, two of which were especially gratifying. The first was an honorary S.D. degree from Harvard with a citation reading "Distinguished physician, Harvard teacher, imaginative experimentalist; his ear is ever attuned to the heartbeat of mankind." The second was the establishment of the Herrman Ludwig Blumgart Professorship of Medicine by his friends, patients, colleagues, and other members of the Beth Israel family.

Though formally retired, he was appointed special consultant to the dean of the Medical School with duties related to the Admissions Committee. During his ten years with this group, his perceptiveness and understanding of contemporary youth led him to emphasize attributes favoring acceptance rather than flaws calling for rejection. His thoroughness while conducting the interviews in a relaxed atmosphere earned the appreciation of the applicants, just as his clear, logical summation and wise judgment were valued by his associates. In his other new role, as consultant physician to the Harvard medical area, he maintained his relationship with students while undertaking a new function, the primary care of patients, a long-cherished goal which had eluded him during his earlier medical career.

In the summer of 1973, he suffered a cerebrovascular accident. The resulting aphasia affected both his speech and his comprehension of spoken language. As Professor Paul Freund has commented, "This master of words whose voice was music, who ranged easily from precision to playfulness in his talk, now found the talent lodged in him useless. Like the merest child, he set about, under devoted tutelage, laboriously relearning a vocabulary until in time he once again could communicate. It was a painful triumph, his final act of dedication and resolve, achieved with the indispensable support of Margaret and their daughter, Ann, whose very name made his face light up like the sun." This illness brought an end to his active and distinguished medical career, though he remained until his last days a figure of impressive bearing, elegant manner and characteristic galantry.

With the devoted guidance of his nephew, Ernest Kahn, M.D. '44, he renewed an interest in art which was earlier demonstrated in his vivid photographs in India of people, architecture, and landscapes. He now channeled his visual perceptiveness into exploring the art treasures of Boston's museums with the same intensity and gratification that had characterized his involvement with people.

His bibliography includes more than 160 papers describing his clinical and laboratory research. Among many scientific contributions are the important observations on the cardiovascular effects of hypothyroidism, induced by surgery or radioactive iodine administration in patients with congestive heart failure or angina pectoris. The clinical, pharmacological and physiological byproducts of his work were many, including important insights into the treatment of hyperthyroidism with radioactive iodine. His work on the coronary circulation was classic. A technique developed by Dr. Monroe J. Schlesinger for the injection and dissection of the coronary arteries led to the joint studies undertaken by Drs. Blumgart and Schlesinger and their associates. Their work constitutes the basis for our present understanding of the anatomy, pathology, and clinical manifestations of coronary angiography and bypass surgery. They demonstrated the importance of the coronary collateral circulation and explained many previous disparities between the clinical manifestations and the pathologic events of coronary occlusion and myocardial infarction.

As a medical statesman, he wrote meaningfully about such subjects as the care of the patient, the training of the physician, and problems of human experimentation. Only those, however, fortunate enough to have known him as colleague, house officer, student, patient, or friend knew the full flavor and influence of the man. To quote a former student, "His true greatness rested not only in his numerous scientific achievements, but also in his radiation of a whole constellation of personal qualities that few men are blessed with, combining a keen vigorous mind with a firm and gentle manner, a lively teacher and a devoted scientist, but above all, and at all times, a gentleman as if by instinct."

He was on the editorial board of many publications, including *The New England Journal of Medicine*. He was a member of the Association of American Physicians, the American Society of Clinical Investigation, the American Physiological Society, and the American Academy of Arts and Sciences.

He served as president of the Harvard Medical School Alumni Association, the Massachusetts Heart Association and the New England Cardiovascular Society. The American Heart Association honored him with the Gold Heart Award for his contributions to cardiology.

Among the named lectureships he was invited to give, the one which meant most to him was the George Washington Gay Lecture on Medical Ethics presented at the Medical School in 1963. He chose for his title "Caring for the Patient," influenced by the closing sentence of Dr. Peabody's own lecture of 1927, one of the most expressive and poignant sentences in modern medical literature—"The secret of the care of the patient is in caring for the patient." Francis Peabody was probably the greatest single influence in shaping his career. As Dr. Blumgart said, "He was my mentor in my fourth-year clerkship, in my first published research, in my internship, and later my chief at the Thorndike Memorial Laboratory." This lecture represents Dr. Blumgart's credo in which he beautifully illustrates the wide range of his thinking and practice, his wisdom, humility, compassion, and joy in his work. His own closing sentence is a paraphrase in reverse of Francis Peabody's, stating that "the secret of caring for the patient is, indeed, to care for the patient."

He advocated a way of life which William Osler had set forth for himself. "I have had three personal ideals; one, to do the day's work well and not worry about tomorrow; second, to act the golden rule as far as in me lay, towards my professional brethren and towards the patients committed to my care; and third has been to cultivate such a measure of equanimity as would enable me to bear success with humility, the affection of my friends without pride, and to be ready when the day of sorrows and grief came to meet it with the courage befitting a man."

Herrman Blumgart lived this way of life.

A. Clifford Barger   Howard H. Hiatt
William B. Castle   Arthur J. Linenthal
A. Stone Freedberg   Paul M. Zoll
Milton W. Hamolsky   Louis Zetzel, *Chairman*

Memorial Minute
Faculty of Medicine
Februrary 24, 1978

VII. Aspirations

HISTORIAN OF PHILOSOPHY

"Within his purview the entire history of philosophy"

HARRY AUSTRYN WOLFSON

November 2, 1887 - September 24, 1974

The quintessential Wolfson, one of this century's great and creative humanists, was well described in the citation accompanying the honorary degree which Harvard conferred upon him in 1956: "From enormous knowledge, he graciously illumines the major problems of religious philosophy and their relations to revealed truth."

Harry Austryn Wolfson was born in the small town of Ostrin, Lithuania, a place-name which he later nostalgically adopted as his personal middle name. His youthful years were spent in various schools of Lithuania where he acquired an intensive, classical Jewish education. Upon his arrival with his family in New York (September, 1903), he continued his Jewish studies and shortly thereafter (1905) settled in Scranton, Pennsylvania, where, at the age of 18, he enrolled in the Central High School and graduated three years later, supporting himself during this period by part-time Hebrew teaching.

A $250 scholarship, awarded on the basis of competitive exams, enabled him to come to Harvard, where tuition was then an exorbitant $150. He quickly and methodically immersed himself in intensive study of history and philosophy. From September 1908, when he arrived in Cambridge, to September 1974, when he died in Stillman Infirmary, this was his home in every sense. His life was totally, inextricably intertwined with Harvard, from which he received his A.B. in 1911, A.M. in 1912, and PH.D. in 1915 and which he left only for two years (1912-14) to enjoy the benefits of a Sheldon Traveling Fellowship in Europe and for five months on military service at Fort Slocum (starting in September, 1918). After several years as a junior faculty member, all along toying with the idea of a literary career, he became, from 1925 to 1958, the first Nathan Littauer Professor of Hebrew Literature and Philosophy. He was honorary curator of Widener's Hebraica Collection, which he himself organized.

He loved Harvard—purely, simply, and without defensiveness—the Harvard of Santayana, James and Royce, of Toy, Jewett, Lyon and Moore, Rand and Woods, and, as the years unfolded, the Harvard of their successors and peers. He was at first awed, then stimulated and challenged by the Harvard tradition, and finally determined to sustain and, we may now say, enhance this great tradition. Much of his work, including selection of fields of research, was inspired by a desire to contribute to general culture in what he conceived to be the universal Harvard tradition.

His many, justly celebrated volumes are monuments to the pertinacity, perspicacity and profundity of his life's work: *Crescas' Critique of Aristotle: Problems of Aristotle's Physics in Jewish and Arabic Philosophy* (1929); *The Philosophy of Spinoza: Unfolding the Latent Processes of His Reasoning*, 2 vols. (1934); *Philo: Foundations of Religious Philosophy in Judaism, Christianity and Islam*, 2 vols. (1947); *The Philosophy of the Church Fathers* (1956); *The Philosophy of Kalam* (1976); and *Repercussions of the Kalam in Jewish Philosophy* (1979). There were, in addition, three collections of papers and articles: *Religious Philosophy*

(1961); *Studies in the History of Philosophy and Religion*, 2 vols. (1973 and 1975). Each one of these large tomes, each one in its own right, could and would be a scholar's pride; each one would amply justify a lifetime devoted exclusively to Hellenistic, or to patristic, or to Islamic, or to scholastic, or to Jewish scholarship.

This is the real measure of Harry Wolfson, of his intellectual daring and imaginativeness; starting as a student of medieval Jewish philosophy, he burst the recognized bounds and bonds of specialized, sometimes provincial scholarship and then patiently but vigorously brought within his purview the entire history of philosophy, moving with verve and aplomb and delicacy from pre-Socratics to neo-Kantians, from Greek atomists to American pragmatists. This tireless scholar was able to combine unflagging attention to detail—stylistic, structural, or substantive—with original powers of synthesis. While elucidating difficult texts and knotty passages, he also clearly formulated a new, anti-Hegelian scheme for the periodization of the history of philosophy—in which Jewish philosophy from Philo to Spinoza was crucial—and expounded, more allusively, a philosophy of the history of philosophy—in which religious thought played a major role.

His files, which he left to Harvard along with the residue of his estate, contain many unpublished works: (1) a volume on Greek philosophy, planned as the introduction to the series on "Structure and Growth of Philosophic Systems from Plato to Spinoza"; (2) the second volume of the *Church Fathers*; and (3) a third volume on Spinoza. The existence of this material in manuscript, along with scores of articles, underscores the dynamism of Wolfson's scholarship. This is reflected also in the constant revision, extending to galley and page proofs, of his publications which annoyed all but the most patient of publishers—Harvard University Press. The printed words, in turn, were preceded by an unremitting, but effortless, oral restatement of his views to visitors in Widener, colleagues at the Faculty Club, and students and friends on long walks around Harvard Square. Through what seemed to be primarily monologues, he kept trying his formulations and discoveries on others as well as on himself.

Moreover, his unrelenting work led him to constant refinement as well as periodic reformulation and defense of his method of minute textual-philological study—what he called the hypothetico-deductive method or the method of conjecture and verification and what was in essence the traditional Talmudic method. While his critics sometimes found him to be too speculative in his unfolding of latent processes of philosophic reasoning, ready to build upon soaring conjecture without sufficient, self-evident textual verification—and it is the daring of his method which contributes both to the solidity as well as the vulnerability of his achievement—he could only retort that the alternative was deadly, stultifying, or prosaic. The following rejoinder to some critical comments is typical: "But all this is based, of course, only upon circumstantial evidence; we have no direct testimony of either al-Kindi or Israeli that this is exactly how their minds worked; bread-and-butter scholarship may, therefore, brush it all aside and dismiss it as unconvincing." His own erudition and ingenuity prevented him from being prosaic or timid.

Wolfson's importance for philosophic scholarship transcended his impressive literary productivity. On one hand, while participating in and contributing to so many areas of scholarship, he could be a forceful, trenchant critic of scholarly fads, conventional views, fashionable schools, flashy academic jargon, and facile explanations which obfuscate rather than illuminate. On the other hand, his personal involvement in certain scholarly fields—Islamic philosophy and theology for example—encouraged students to devote their energies to them. Wolfson's trailblazing investigation of Averroes led to the preparation of a "Plan for the Publication of a *Corpus Commentariorum Averrois in Aristotelem,*" which in turn goaded and guided other scholars to edit these commentaries of Averroes, the great Islamic philosopher whom Wolfson dubbed "a naturalized Hebrew and Latin author."

As first incumbent of the first chair in an American university fully devoted to Jewish studies, he played an important role in the instutionalization and profession-alization of Jewish studies and their spread across the American campus.

His classroom performance—in Emerson Hall or on the top floor of Widener—was a paradigm of excellence and skill in teaching, a real experience of higher educa-tion. He was a Socratic teacher who made use of Aristo-telian catharsis.

His quasi-ascetic regimen notwithstanding—his long hours in Widener, his reluctantly confirmed bachelor-hood, his never going on vacation—he was not a recluse. The cinema and, later, television were his favorite relax-ations; he particularly enjoyed what he called Ameri-cana—no foreign films for him. He drew strength from the old Harvard Square; dining out was a joy as well as a necessity. Most notably, he was a wise and under-standing counselor of students (and younger colleagues), not only concerning curricular problems and dilemmas of concentration, research, placement and publication, but also concerning personal problems, including mar-riage. He was gracious and unstinting, refreshing and challenging, in guiding and advising, as well as in sharing his erudition and insight.

The scholarly legacy of Harry Wolfson—philosophical perceptivity and philological precision—is rich and stimulating.

Burton S. Dreben   Muhsin S. Mahdi
Richard N. Frye   George H. Williams
        Isadore Twersky, *Chairman*

Memorial Minute
Faculty of Arts and Sciences
May 6, 1975

LEGAL SCHOLAR

"Exemplar of civic virtue and moral courage"

MARK DeWOLFE HOWE

May 22, 1906 - February 28, 1967

Mark Howe used to speculate that he was destined by inheritance to live into a long, enveloping evening of deepening shadows until the final darkness would fall as an ultimate benediction. What grim irony in that foreboding! He lived his life in sunlight and the passing clouds of morning and a bright  afternoon; then a sudden sunset and the radiance of an afterglow.

Touched with fire, he lived a life of quiet heroism. He had learned early from Justice Holmes that:

> Only when you have worked alone—when you have felt around you a black gulf of solitude more isolating than that which surrounds the dying man, and in hope and in despair have trusted to your own unshaken will—then only will you have achieved. Thus only can you gain the secret isolated joy of the thinker, who knows that a hundred years after he is dead and forgotten, men who never heard of him will be moving to the measure of his thought.

In his magisterial work on Holmes himself—the resourcefully edited letters and diary and speeches, the

two magnificent biographical volumes of the shaping and
the proving years, and the brilliantly illuminating introduction to *The Common Law*—Mark succeeded in the
heroic feat of reliving the intellectual life of another
without losing his own identity or vitality. He experi-
enced the secret isolated joy of fathoming a mind of
another generation and making it luminously accessible
to the generations that will follow. Any visitor who pen-
etrated the barricades of books that were Mark's office
and examined the row on row of volumes that Holmes
had recorded as his own reading must have marveled that
so complete an absorption into the mind of another could
be achieved without a transmigration of the soul; but on
looking further into the fortress of his study you would
have been surrounded by volumes and manuscripts on
American colonial history, on church and state, on civil
rights, on contemporary legislation and proposals and
hearings, attesting, all of them, to the unique reality,
the vital identity of Mark Howe.

To write meaningfully of a great man requires qualities
of greatness in the biographer. Mark Howe possessed
greatness of heart as well as of mind. In the law school
community he was not merely our surest guide to the
ideas and institutions of the American heritage; he was
our unfailing and unflinching exemplar of civic virtue
and moral courage.

The temptation is irresistible to think of him as the
finest flowering of New England Puritanism. It was a
Puritanism nourished by his absorption in the early history of New England that led to some of his most fastidious scholarship, that produced the volume he called *The
Garden and the Wilderness*, in which he pressed the claim
that the evangelicalism of Roger Williams, concerned
with the purity of the church's garden, was as much
responsible for the first amendment as the political sec-
ularism of Thomas Jefferson. He was in truth a Puritan
in his deep sense of stewardship, his sensitivity to duty,
his sternness with himself. But it was a Puritanism tem-
pered by the sweetness and gentleness of his nature, a

shy, puckish humor, and a playful skepticism that showed itself in the blue-eyed candor with which he punctured most absolutes and all pretentiousness.

Those of us who collaborated with him on a casebook found these qualities a comfort and a delight. Shouldering more than his share of the joint enterprise, he composed most of the biographical sketches of the justices that gave the book whatever flavor it had. Of Chief Justice White, Mark Howe wrote: "He moved portentously across the thinnest ice, confident that a lifeline of adverbs—'inevitably,' 'irresistibly,' 'clearly,' and 'necessarily'—was supporting him in his progress." Of the first Mr. Justice Harlan: "He . . . could fairly be described by Mr. Justice Brewer as a man who 'goes to bed every night with one hand on the Constitution and the other on the Bible, and so sleeps the sweet sleep of justice and righteousness.' The consequence of such sleep was shown in Hennington v. Georgia, . . . where the Court in an opinion by Harlan sustained a state statute which forbade the movement of freight trains on the Sabbath." Only a very mellow Puritan could have written that.

But in the face of moral obtuseness he was burningly indignant. Just the other day I came across the transcript of a recent conference on civil rights, where the question was raised why so many Negroes hold white men in contempt. There were many explanations proffered, learned and unlearned, when Mark intervened. "The reason is very simple," he said. "We are frauds, and they know it." Only a very angry and compassionate Puritan could have said that.

More and more of late this side of his nature was engaged, as he witnessed and bore witness in the great new emancipation struggle of our time. In the summer of 1966, when others were vacillating between seashore and mountains for retreat, he chose the dust and heat of the Mississippi Delta country, and won the garland of friendship and gratitude from many a humble client whom he counseled and defended.

He was looked to for leadership because he served modestly in the ranks. He won the hearts of the troubled because he did not wear his heart upon his sleeve. In the lives of a generation of students he was profoundly important because they saw that he was not self-important. To them he communicated implicitly a sense of the responsibilities of manhood because he never lost his unaffected boyishness of spirit.

The loss of one who gave so much and had so much to give brings wintry mourning to us all. But it mercifully brings too a quickening spirit of renewal. Our final parting must be words that sound that note, valiant words of Justice Holmes that Mark knew so well and that I like to think Holmes would have wanted said at the last hail and farewell to his and our beloved friend:

> Our dead brothers still live for us, and bid us think of life, not death—of life to which in their youth they lent the passion and glory of the spring. As I listen, the great chorus of life and joy begins again, and amid the awful orchestra of seen and unseen powers and destinies of good and evil our trumpets sound once more a note of daring, hope, and will.

A memoir prepared by Paul A. Freund
Carl M. Loeb University Professor
for the service in Memorial Church, March 3, 1967
and later published in the
Harvard Law Review, 80:1632 (1967).
© *Harvard Law Review.*

PASTOR AND DEAN

*"A pastor who led the Divinity School
into a wider role"*

SAMUEL HOWARD MILLER

February 3, 1900 - March 20, 1968

Samuel Howard Miller was born
in Philadelphia, brought up in
New Jersey, and spent a year at
Massachusetts Institute of
Technology (1917-18). His
interest turned at this time
from engineering to human
relations, and after a move to
enlist in the Marines was interrupted by the Armistice, he

entered Colgate University to take a four-year course
combining theology and general education, leading to
the degree of B.TH., which he completed in 1923. After
graduation from Colgate there followed 12 years of Baptist pastorates in New Jersey: Belmar, 1923-28; Arlington,
1928-30; Clifton, 1930-35.

Samuel Miller came to the pastorate of the Old Cambridge Baptist Church in 1935. The quality of his 24-
year ministry there is reflected not only in the testimony
of his parishioners but in the writings that emerged from
it and the part-time teaching appointments that he
undertook. This period of his ministry is described by
his successor as follows: "After leading his congregation

212

through the continuous crises of the Great Depression, World War II, and finally the institutional crises of a crumbling spire and a dwindling flock (there was a serious move to close the church in 1946), Samuel Miller led his people in an inner renewal of the spirit symbolized by the Memorial Prayer Chapel," almost every detail of which was fashioned by members of the parish under his lead. The Book of Remembrance in the foyer of the Chapel contains a page illuminated by a member of the congregation which well suggests his versatility. "Samuel Howard Miller, tenth minister of the Old Cambridge Baptist Church from 1935 until 1959, was Preacher, Teacher, Ecumenical Leader, Friend and Helper, Counsellor to many, Author, Fosterer of the Arts of Worship, Sponsor of Exhibits in Religious Art, Inspirer and Instructor of Theological Students, Versatile and Energetic both manually and mentally."

Samuel Miller was adjunct professor of the philosophy of religion at the Andover Newton Theological School from 1951 on, for seven years. His role at the Harvard Divinity School began in 1954 as lecturer. He became professor of pastoral theology in 1958, the year before his appointment as dean and John Lord O'Brian Professor in succession to Douglas Horton. Although he bypassed the A.B. degree and had no graduate training, his wide reading and realistic immersion in the tasks of the modern church and an innate critical sense combined to equip him for distinguished religious leadership. He was a master of the spiritual life. His ministry, both in church and school, was enriched by his long initiation into the arts, both in the exercise of his own diverse talents— painting, modeling, stained glass, linoleum prints—and in his profound concern with the symbolics of the church and the age. He prepared librettos for oratorios, performed at national assemblies of his denomination and on other occasions. He was secretary of the Department of Worship and the Arts of the National Council of Churches.

213

All these talents he brought to the deanship of the Divinity School in 1959. In his case as in that of Willard Sperry in 1922, Harvard did the unusual in calling a man out of the pastoral ministry as head of a university seminary. The particular tasks confronting the school at this time made the choice all the more felicitous. Its endowment had recently been strengthened and the faculty and student body rebuilt, but the major task remained of redefining theological goals and curriculum so as to relate them to our revolutionary era. During his administration the school maintained and advanced its position as one of the very few top centers of graduate study of religion in the country, and at the same time effected a breakthrough in the modernizing of professional training, especially in connection with the establishment of a Department of the Church. It was, therefore, also enabled to move into wider ecumenical and scholarly leadership beyond the University. The school made history in 1963 with the Roman Catholic-Protestant Colloquium, attended by Cardinal Bea—the first major American response to the Second Vatican Council. This was followed by a notable Jewish-Christian Colloquium in 1966. The school was co-sponsor of the International Conference on Abortion in Washington in 1967. Various internship programs and interdisciplinary activities within the University are further legacies of the dean's concern for involving the school in the life of the churches and society.

Dean Miller was the author of seven volumes. The publication date of the last of these, *Religion in a Technological Age*, coincided with the date of his death. This volume bearing the imprint of the Harvard University Press was dedicated by the author to his colleagues in the Harvard Divinity School. He received honorary degrees from seven institutions. He was secretary for years of the Boston Ministers' Club. He had a very wide reception on the lecture platform, and because of the many dimensions of his outreach he was able to arrest the attention of circles that had become disaffiliated from the church and to interest them in the new programs of the school.

Before his death he had the satisfaction of seeing long-standing needs of the school met by major gifts. The faculty, staff and other friends, moreover, installed in the library in his honor a modern stained-glass window by Joseph C. Ferguson in anticipation of his imminent retirement. It was dedicated at Commencement after his death.

Samuel Miller's theological stance and religious power owed much to an old Baptist and Anabaptist spirituality, enriched by mystics and poets ancient and modern, Christian and secular. It was this kinship which made current neo-orthodoxy as well as some forms of pragmatic American churchmanship uncongenial to him. His engagement with the contemporary world was all the more responsible and effective because he was able, like Paul Tillich, to recognize the latent church and to appreciate the secular quests of the time. This appeared in his writing and teaching as he entered into dialogue with contemporary artists and writers, but it also informed his practical strategies for theological education and the work of the church. It was therefore especially appropriate that the faculty, staff, alumni, and friends of the Divinity School establish the Samuel Howard Miller Fund envisaged for the school's work in the field of pastoral psychology. This fund perpetuates his name and furthers the concerns which he cherished.

J. Lawrence Burkholder Herbert Gezork
Harvey G. Cox Wayne W. Horvath
Amos N. Wilder, *Chairman*

Memorial Minute
Faculty of Divinity
October 18, 1968

PHILOSOPHER OF EDUCATION

*"Reverence for educational concerns and a
commitment to serve others"*

ROBERT ULICH

April 21, 1890 - June 17, 1977

Robert Ulich was invited in
1933 by Dean Henry Wyman
Holmes of the Harvard Graduate School of Education for a
one-year lectureship. Under the
increasingly oppressive circumstances in Germany, Ulich was
eager to accept the invitation,
leaving in January of 1934 to
begin his Harvard career.

Appointed to a professorship later in 1934, named James
Bryant Conant Professor of Education in 1954, he lectured and wrote mainly on the philosophy and history of
education and on comparative education. After his retirement in 1961, he continued writing and returned period-
ically to Germany. In 1970 he left the United States
permanently, becoming a resident of the Augustinum in
Stuttgart, where he died.

Born in Riedemühl bei Lam in Bavaria, he at one stage
in his higher education considered entering the ministry.
He received a classical, historical, and philosophical
education in several German universities and obtained
his PH.D. from the University of Leipzig in 1915, his

dissertation being on Christian Friedrich Scherenberg, a contribution to the history of nineteenth-century literature. In 1918 he married Else Beil, a political activist and fellow doctoral student, whose dissertation in the same year as his was on the development of the concept of world literature. Robert Ulich served at several levels of education and educational administration, becoming counselor (*Ministerialrat*) of higher education for Saxony (1920-33) and professor in the philosophical faculty at the Dresden Institute of Technology (1927-33). His poetic urge had found expression in his translation of the *Carmina Burana* (June 1927).

In 1929 Ulich married the daughter of the wartime Swedish ambassador to St. Petersburg, Elsa Brändström (1888-1948), called "The Angel of Siberia" for her resourceful organization of relief for prisoners of war. Just a year before the accession of Hitler to power, Ulich had outlined an important reconceptualization of the role of the institutes of technology (*Technische Hochschulen*) in the Weimar Republic (Berlin, 1932). Courageously, the sometime Ministerialrat Ulich and the Swedish-born heroine of mercy for former German and Austrian prisoners in the First World War were equally determined to leave Hitler's Germany. Elsa Ulich became the second president of the Window Shop on Brattle Street, the complex of activities designed to provide gainful employment for refugees from Nazism like themselves.

A scholar with an administrative past, a historian and philosopher with poetic gifts and deep religious sensibilities, Robert Ulich brought a cultivated and wide-ranging mind to bear on the subjects he taught at Harvard. His poetic writings served, along with his formal scholarly work, to sustain his unusual capacities for growth in awareness and appreciation of life's values in the midst of trouble. In 1971, he wrote of his poetry, "Without this form of self-expression, I might not have survived the cruel calamities of my life—the rise of the Nazis, the forced emigration, and the destruction of some

217

of my most cherished plans for the future of German higher education."

During his academic life at Harvard, Ulich made distinguished contributions through his extensive writings and his teaching. He was a leader in developing the fields of comparative education and the history of educational thought; he taught the history of universities in the Faculty of Arts and Sciences and the history of religious education at the Divinity School; he published important works on the theory of democratic secondary education; and he worked out a comprehensive idealistic philosophy in his book *The Human Career* (1955), which expressed his abiding faith in the capacities of human beings for continued self-transcendence.

Because of Ulich's breadth of interests he in due course found himself a welcomed frequenter of the Faculty Club at the "legendary table of disparate scholars," long associated with the late Harry A. Wolfson. From the period of his career in Germany, Ulich was a friend of Paul Tillich and was in a position to welcome him when the latter was appointed University Professor at Harvard.

Ulich maintained a characteristic scholarly reserve vis-a-vis the scientific and progressivist tendencies dominant in American educational theory. It is not that he was opposed to empiricism, but that he considered the prevalent school of educational empiricists to be philosophically shallow and historically naive. "I fully agreed with John Dewey," he wrote, "that we have to replace older dogmatic views, be they philosophical or religious in nature, by a more dynamic and empirical outlook toward the problems of life and man. But to make a new dogma out of 'empiricism'. . . I simply asked the question: How can man be empirical; how can he invent and use instruments, physical as well as intellectual; and how can he experiment within a systematic sequence of ideas and with some hope of success? Only by transcending his subjective self towards a greater self . . . Thus, in my first book on educational philosophy, *Fundamentals of Democratic Education* (1940), I coined the awkward phrase 'self-transcendent empiricism,' nevertheless the best I could find."

And in response to what he considered the grave historical inadequacy of American educational theory, he produced his *History of Educational Thought* (1945), his influential collection *Three Thousand Years of Educational Widsom* (1947), and his comparative study *The Education of Nations* (1961). In these works, and especially in the anthology of 1947, his longtime friend Hedwig Schleiffer of Vienna, long since of Cambridge, was an acknowledged research assistant, as also Mary Ewen Palmer, whom he later married. Ulich's purpose in these books was to place the process of education in a broad cultural, intellectual, and historical setting. His aim was, as he put it, "to prove that those men who determined the course of Western education were not merely concerned with schools and with didactic methods, but were great thinkers and often courageous reformers. Most of them harbored a profoundly mystical trend (even Dewey, despite all his struggles against it). Education for them was a continual process of the examination, transmission, and reformation of human values, and most of all, a process of inspiration."

In 1965, Ulich appeared jointly with Professor Paul A. Freund in a small book that grew out of Inglis lectures at the Graduate School of Education, dealing with a major issue in American secondary education: *Religion and the Public Schools: The Legal and the Educational Issue.* Growing in part out of his courses in the Divinity School, beginning in 1955, was his project of an anthology of documents eventually published as *A History of Religious Education from the Judaeo-Christian Tradition* (1967).

Despite, or perhaps because of, his philosophical independence, Ulich's educational influence was significant if indirect, and much of his criticism of prevailing trends has outlasted the enthusiastic conformism they generated. Much of his influence was channeled through his Harvard students and advisees. He attracted, over the years, a large number of doctoral students who, though "they never became his 'disciples,'. . . did share a kind of pragmatic idealism. . . ." They "went on to serve American education in many capacities, yet each bore in some way his own idiosyncratic version of Ulich's reverence for intellectual concerns and his commitment to serve others." These words themselves were penned by one of those many Harvard alumni who became known as "Ulich students."

Before leaving America for the last time, Ulich had in press *Progress or Disaster: From the Bourgeois to the World Citizen,* returning to a theme of his first wife on the essence of a world literature. Back in Germany, he bethought himself also of his second wife in a series of poems originally dedicated to Elsa Brändström for her last years, entitled *Das grosse Geheimnis* (1970) and shortly before, also in German, he published poems on man and the cosmos.

In all of his writings, Ulich exhibited a characteristic breadth of perspective, locating the educational process within a historical framework of social and intellectual development as well as a comparative scheme in which national differences were revealed for reflection. He provided for Harvard and for education in general an admirable model of humanistic scholarship, pursued steadfastly and independently under the guidance of an inspiring philosophical vision.

Israel Scheffler   George H. Williams
Francis Keppel, *Chairman*

Memorial Minute
Faculties of Divinity and Education
May 15 and 17, 1978

CRITIC AND TEACHER

"Enormous influence on the study of literature and language"

IVOR ARMSTRONG RICHARDS

February 26, 1893 - September 7, 1979

Ivor Armstrong Richards, University Professor, was one of this century's great humanists and interpreters of literature, as well as an innovative theorist in linguistics and in education generally. Born in Sandbach, Cheshire, England, he attended Clifton College and then took first class honors in moral sciences (1915) at Magdalene College, Cambridge, with a special emphasis on logic and psychology. Receiving his M.A. in 1918, he continued his study of psychology, supplemented by work in physiology and medicine, and for a time planned to become a psychoanalyst. But his interest in the uses of literature and his gift as a teacher continued to deepen. In 1922 he became a lecturer in English and Moral Sciences at Cambridge and in 1926 fellow of Magdalene College. Meanwhile he took an active part in developing the new Cambridge program of English studies which was later to serve as an inspiration for critics and scholars throughout the English-speaking world.

Threatened with tuberculosis as a youth, Richards had taken up mountaineering for a hobby in order to strengthen his health. While mountaineering in Wales in 1916, he met his future wife, Dorothea Pilley, a noted alpinist. Married in 1926, the two devoted 30 seasons to climbing the Alps, 7 in the Canadian Rockies, 2 in the Himalayas, and, after coming to Harvard, they made innumerable excursions in the mountains of northern New England. Some of their earlier experiences are related in Mrs. Richards' book, *Climbing Days* (1935).

Richards, who enjoyed travel, was especially fascinated by the Orient, and in 1927 he lectured in Japan and traveled across India. Reflecting his interest in Chinese thought and expression is his book, *Mencius on the Mind* (1932), written largely in China (1929-31) while he was serving as visiting professor at Tsing Hua University and at the Peking National University. He stopped at Harvard for a term, on his way home, to serve as visiting lecturer in English (1931); he returned to Harvard eight years later as lecturer in education (1939) and director of the Commission on English Language Studies. In 1944 he was appointed university professor. During the war years he was an active member of the committee that designed the General Education program, and in 1947 and 1948 gave the first half of Humanities 1, in which he concentrated on Homer, Plato, and the Old Testament ("The three big B.C.s" as he called them).

It is a commonplace that important works in the humanities, as contrasted with the systematic sciences, rarely have an immediate impact. Since they appeal not through exact demonstration but to general observation and experience, it takes time for them to sink in (or unusual perception at the start to see their promise). Richards had a precocious talent, and during his late twenties and early thirties wrote works that took another 10 to 15 years, at least, to create the widespread effect they ultimately had on the study both of literature and the psychology of language: *The Meaning of Meaning* (1922), written in collaboration with the polymath C.K.

Ogden, *Science and Poetry* (1925), and, above all, his *Principles of Literary Criticism* (1924), published when he was 31, and *Practical Criticism* (1929), published when he was 36. Three further works of criticism, written during the next decade, both modify and extend premises outlined in these earlier works: *Coleridge on Imagination* (1934), and his more linguistically oriented books, *The Philosophy of Rhetoric* (1936), and *Interpretation in Teaching* (1938).

As a literary critic, Richards returned to the British eighteenth-century and romantic tradition of empirical and psychological analysis, which had focused on the imaginative process. He tried to give it a new scientific basis. In addition he concentrated on the nature of communication and the connotative power of words. In his *Practical Criticism*, after revealing the often grotesque misreading by students when confronted by poems not already identified and discussed for them, he advocated (and exemplified) the value of focusing on the text to the comparative exclusion of other considerations that had dominated literary study. He felt that conventional literary history, antiquarianism, the study of sources, and the use of biographical and historical background, had taken precedence over close encounters with the text. As a countermeasure he urged the approach to a poem as an artifact, with special attention to metaphor, symbol, imagery, and associational implication and to the organic interrelation of the parts into the whole. Here especially he was to prove influential in the approach of the famous "new criticism," which became so widespread in universities after World War II. From his own point of view, this innovator was conservative in his aim. His purpose was to reassert and give further strength to the ancient classical belief that art, at its best, can act formatively in enlarging sensibility, deepening sympathies, and developing a more organized and harmonious ability to experience life. We should add that his brilliance as a critic, like that of his hero, Samuel Taylor Coleridge, resulted from the sheer range and diversity of his interests.

In summing up his career as a critic, a word should be added about his teaching. In tutorial and small classes, he was kindly, suggestive, full of ideas, quick to get the student's point of view. But where he excelled was as a lecturer. He could dazzle crowds of listeners—who would hang upon every word—from members of the Harvard faculty to a class of 700 in Sanders Theatre. Perhaps because of his Welsh background, he was unrivaled in reading poetry aloud. So hypnotic was the effect that, as his friend T.S. Eliot said, Richards could read aloud a telephone directory and make it sound like Dante or Shakespeare. The ability to lecture and to read so marvelously remained with him into extreme old age; and in his eighties, students by the hundred would crowd the Loeb Theatre to hear him read and explicate a mere three or four poems.

The later teaching and writing of Richards, aside from occasional works and lectures in literary interpretation, and a course on poetics (1959-62), reveal the continuing interplay of three major interests: semantics, or the study of meaning and implication in and through words; the psychology of education, in both the humanities and sciences, from the primary to the universal level; and the possibilities of the international communication of cultures. The combination of all three of these concerns led him to champion and develop his friend Ogden's concept of "Basic English," in the hope of creating an international language through the use of 850 carefully selected words. In his own translations into "Basic," it is typical that he chose selections from such formidable writers as Homer and Plato in order to show what could be done. Meanwhile, he gave early and crucial support to creative applications of psychology and linguistics to teaching, programmed instruction and testing.

Of the many books that he wrote, collaborated on, or edited after 1940, space forbids mention of more than a few: *How to Read a Page* (1942), *Basic English and Its Uses* (1943), *Speculative Instruments* (1955), and with Christine

Gibson and others, some manuals on teaching the fundamentals of different languages, with the help of pictures. In addition to some short plays (*Job's Comforter; A Leak in the Universe; Tomorrow Morning, Faustus!*), he turned his hand to lyric verse and produced three volumes in his sixties and seventies, having hardly ever written verse before: *Goodbye Earth and Other Poems* (1958), *The Screens and Other Poems* (1960), and a general collection, *Internal Colloquies* (1971). The style is gnomic, succinct, neatly constructed; and the moods are elegiac, cosmic, and detached. He of course viewed his late excursion into verse as one of many appendices to a long and varied career. As he grew older, he became more pluralistic, speaking not of "knowledge" but of "knowledges." So, when his early *Science and Poetry* was reissued years later, it was called *Poetries and Sciences* (1970).

Honors, in his last 30 years, fell on him like a February snow in the northern New England he loved. After his retirement (1963), he remained in Cambridge, Massachusetts, writing, lecturing, occasionally mountaineering, for another eleven years. In 1974 he and his wife moved back to his native Cambridge, where they lived adjacent to Magdalene College. But the Richardses continued to return each fall to New England—first to the New Hampshire mountains and then to Harvard. In April 1979, at the age of 86, he again paid a visit to Peking, where he lectured at the university, and helped to set up a pilot study to solve the vast training problems confronting China. Taken ill in June, he was tended for some weeks by an admiring China, and finally, in a special plane, flown back to Cambridge, where he died.

Jeanne Chall
Russell Davis
John H. Finley
Christine Gibson

Francis Keppel
Harry Levin
David Perkins
W. Jackson Bate, *Chairman*

Memorial Minute
Faculty of Arts and Sciences
April 23, 1980